new interchange

English for international communication

Jack C. Richards

INTRO

student's book

CAMBRIDGE
UNIVERSITY PRESS

CAMBRIDGE UNIVERSITY PRESS
Cambridge, New York, Melbourne, Madrid, Cape Town, Singapore, São Paulo, Delhi

Cambridge University Press
32 Avenue of the Americas, New York, NY 10013–2473, USA

www.cambridge.org
Information on this title: www.cambridge.org/9780521773997

First published 2000
26th printing 2008

New Interchange Intro Student's Book has been developed from *Interchange* Intro
Student's Book, first published by Cambridge University Press in 1994

Printed in Hong Kong, China, by Golden Cup Printing Company Limited

A catalog record for this publication is available from the British Library

Library of Congress Cataloging in Publication data
Richards, Jack C.
New interchange: English for international communication :
intro student's book / Jack C. Richards.
p.cm.
ISBN 978-0-521-77399-7 (pbk)
1. English language – Textbooks for foreign speakers.
2. Communication, International – Problems, exercises, etc. I. Title.
PE1128.R4588 2000
428.2'4 – dc21   99-059757

ISBN 978-0-521-77399-7 Intro Student's Book
ISBN 978-0-521-77398-0 Intro Student's Book A
ISBN 978-0-521-77397-3 Intro Student's Book B
ISBN 978-0-521-77390-4 Intro Workbook
ISBN 978-0-521-77389-8 Intro Workbook A
ISBN 978-0-521-77388-1 Intro Workbook B
ISBN 978-0-521-77391-1 Intro Teacher's Edition
ISBN 978-0-521-77387-4 Intro Teacher's Manual
ISBN 978-0-521-77386-7 Intro Class Audio Cassettes
ISBN 978-0-521-77385-0 Intro Student's Audio Cassette A
ISBN 978-0-521-77384-3 Intro Student's Audio Cassette B
ISBN 978-0-521-77375-1 Intro Class Audio CDs
ISBN 978-0-521-77374-4 Intro Student's Audio CD A
ISBN 978-0-521-77373-7 Intro Student's Audio CD B
ISBN 978-0-521-65913-0 Intro Audio Sampler–3

Also available
ISBN 978-0-521-55574-6 Intro Video (NTSC)
ISBN 978-0-521-62964-5 Intro Video (PAL)
ISBN 978-0-521-62965-2 Intro Video (SECAM)
ISBN 978-0-521-55573-9 Intro Video Activity Book
ISBN 978-0-521-55572-2 Intro Video Teacher's Guide
ISBN 978-0-521-63887-6 Intro Video Sampler 1–2
ISBN 978-0-521-00008-6 CD-ROM (PC & MAC format)
ISBN 978-0-521-77383-6 Intro Lab Guide
ISBN 978-0-521-77382-9 Intro Lab Cassettes
ISBN 978-0-521-80575-9 Teacher-Training Video with
                        Video Manual
ISBN 978-0-521-62882-2 New Interchange/Passages
                        Placement and Evaluation Package

Book design, art direction, and layout services: Adventure House, NYC
Illustrators: Adventure House, Daisy de Puthod, Randy Jones, Wally Neibert, Roger Roth, Bill Thomson,
Daniel Vasconcellos, Sam Viviano
Photo researchers: Sylvia P. Bloch, Adventure House

Introduction

THE NEW EDITION

New Interchange is the second edition of *Interchange*, one of the world's most successful and popular English courses. *New Interchange* incorporates suggestions from around the world, offered by students and teachers using the first edition. Some major changes include many new Conversations, Snapshots, and Readings; more extensive Grammar Focus models and activities; a greater variety and amount of listening materials; and extensive changes to the **Teacher's Edition** and **Workbook**. This Student's Book includes fresh new content, more visuals to introduce vocabulary, more opportunities to build fluency, and up-to-date art and design.

New Interchange is a multi-level course in English as a second or foreign language for young adults and adults. The course covers the four skills of listening, speaking, reading, and writing, as well as improving pronunciation and building vocabulary. Particular emphasis is placed on listening and speaking. The primary goal of the course is to teach the ability to communicate according to the situation, purpose, and roles of the participants. The language used in *New Interchange* is American English; however, the course reflects the fact that English is the major language of international communication and is not limited to any one country, region, or culture. The first level is designed for beginners and for learners needing a thorough review of basic structures and vocabulary. It provides a smooth transition to the remaining levels in the series.

COURSE LENGTH

Each full level of *New Interchange* contains between 70 and 120 hours of class instruction time. For classes where more time is available, the Teacher's Edition gives detailed suggestions for Optional Activities to extend each unit. Where less time is available, the amount of time spent on Interchange Activities, Reading, Optional Activities, and the Workbook can be reduced.

Each split edition contains approximately 35 to 60 hours of classroom material. The Student's Book, Workbook, and Student's Audio Cassettes or CDs are available in split editions.

COURSE COMPONENTS

The **Student's Book** contains 16 six-page units, each divided into two topical/functional "cycles," as well as four review units. At the back of the book are 16 communication tasks, called "Interchange Activities," and summaries of grammar and vocabulary taught in each unit.

The full-color **Teacher's Edition** features detailed teaching instructions directly across from the Student's Book pages, along with audio scripts, cultural notes, answer keys, and optional activities. At the back of the Teacher's Edition are instructions for Interchange Activities, an Optional Activities Index, a Workbook Answer Key, and four photocopiable Achievement Tests with audio scripts and answer keys.

The **Workbook** provides a variety of reading, writing, and spelling exercises to reinforce the grammar and vocabulary taught in the Student's Book. Each six-page unit follows the same teaching sequence as the Student's Book; some exercises recycle teaching points from previous units in the context of the new topic. The Workbook can be used for classwork or homework.

The **Class Audio Program**, available on cassette or CD, is intended for classroom use. The Conversations, Grammar Focus models, Pronunciation exercises, and Listening activities in the Student's Book are all recorded naturally with a variety of native and some nonnative accents. The Class Audio Program for this level of *New Interchange* also provides recordings of all Readings and of many Snapshots and Word Power sections. Recorded exercises are indicated with the symbol ▣.

The **Student's Audio Program** provides opportunities for self-study. It contains recordings of all Student's Book exercises marked with the symbol ▣, except for the Listening tasks, which are intended only for classroom use. These tasks appear exclusively on the Class Audio Program and are indicated by the symbol CLASS AUDIO ONLY ▶

The **Video** offers entertaining dramatic or documentary sequences that review and extend language learned in each unit of the Student's Book. The **Video Activity Book** contains comprehension, conversation, and language practice activities, and the **Video Teacher's Guide** provides instructional support, answer keys, and photocopiable transcripts of the video sequences.

The **CD-ROM**, appropriate for home or laboratory use, offers a wealth of additional practice. Each of the 16 units is based on a sequence from the Video. Four tests help students monitor their progress.

The **Placement Test** helps determine the most appropriate level of *New Interchange* for incoming students. A booklet contains the four-skills test on photocopiable pages, as well as instructions for test administration and scoring. A cassette accompanies the listening section of the test.

The **Lab Cassettes** provide self-study activities in the areas of grammar, vocabulary, pronunciation, listening, and functional use of English. The **Lab Guide** contains photocopiable pages that guide students through the activities.

The **Teacher-Training Video** offers clear guidance for teaching each section of the Student's Book and professional development activities appropriate for individual or group use.

■ APPROACH AND METHODOLOGY

New Interchange teaches students how to use English for everyday situations and purposes related to school, social life, work, and leisure. The underlying philosophy is that learning a second or foreign language is more rewarding, meaningful, and effective when the language is used for authentic communication. Throughout *New Interchange,* students are presented with natural and useful language. In addition, students have the opportunity to personalize the language they learn, make use of their own knowledge and experiences, and express their ideas and opinions.

■ KEY FEATURES

Adult and International Content *New Interchange* deals with contemporary topics that are of high interest and relevant to both students and teachers. The topics have been selected for their interest to both homogeneous and heterogeneous classes.

Integrated Syllabus *New Interchange* has an integrated, multi-skills syllabus that links topics, communicative functions, and grammar. Grammar – seen as an essential component of second and foreign language proficiency and competence – is always presented communicatively,

with controlled accuracy-based activities leading to fluency-based communicative practice. In this way, there is a link between grammatical form and communicative function. The syllabus is carefully graded, with a gradual progression of teaching items.

Enjoyable and Useful Learning Activities A variety of interesting and enjoyable activities provides thorough individual student practice and enables learners to apply the language they learn. The course also makes extensive use of information-gap tasks; role plays; and pair, group, and whole class activities. Task-based and information-sharing activities provide a maximum amount of student-generated communication.

■ WHAT EACH UNIT CONTAINS

Snapshot The Snapshots graphically present interesting real-world information that introduces the topic of a unit or cycle, and also develop vocabulary. Follow-up questions encourage discussion of the Snapshot material and personalize the topic.

Conversation The Conversations introduce the new grammar of each cycle in a communicative context and present functional and conversational expressions.

Grammar Focus The new grammar of each unit is presented in color boxes and is followed by controlled and freer communicative practice activities. These freer activities often have students use the grammar in a personal context.

Fluency Exercise These pair, group, whole class, or role-play activities provide more personal practice of the new teaching points and increase the opportunity for individual student practice.

Pronunciation These exercises focus on important features of spoken English, including stress, rhythm, intonation, reductions, blending, and sound contrasts.

Listening The Listening activities develop a wide variety of listening skills, including listening for gist, listening for details, and inferring meaning from context. Charts or graphics often accompany these task-based exercises to lend support to students.

Word Power The Word Power activities develop students' vocabulary through a variety of interesting tasks, such as word maps and collocation exercises. Word Power activities are usually followed by oral or written practice that helps students understand how to use the vocabulary in context. Most of these are recorded.

Reading Beginning in Unit 5, there are reading passages designed to develop a variety of reading skills, including reading for details, skimming, scanning, and making inferences. Various text types adapted from authentic sources are included. Also included are pre-reading tasks and post-reading questions that use the topic of the reading as a springboard to discussion.

Writing Writing tasks are integrated throughout each unit within the Grammar Focus practice, Fluency exercises, and Interchange Activities. The writing practice includes practical writing tasks that extend and reinforce the teaching points in the unit.

Interchange Activities The Interchange Activities are pair work, group work, or whole class activities involving information sharing and role playing to encourage real communication. These exercises are a central part of the course and allow students to extend and personalize what they have practiced and learned in each unit.

Unit Summaries Unit Summaries are located at the back of the Student's Book. They contain lists of the key vocabulary and functional expressions for each unit.

Author's Acknowledgments

A great number of people contributed to the development of *New Interchange*. Particular thanks are owed to the following:

The **reviewers** using the first edition of *Interchange* in the following schools and institutes – the insights and suggestions of these teachers and their students have helped define the content and format of the new edition:

Laura Renart, **TS Eliot Bilingual Studies,** Buenos Aires, Argentina; Blanca Arazi and the teachers at **Instituto Cultural Argentino Norteamericano (ICANA),** Buenos Aires, Argentina; Alda Lafeta Toledo, Márcia Soares Guimarães, and the teachers at **ICBEU Belo Horizonte,** Brazil; Jorge Haber Resque, **Centro Cultural Brasil-Estados Unidos (CCBEU),** Belém, Brazil; Mary Oliveira and Montserrat M. Djmal, **Instituto Brasil-Estados Unidos (IBEU),** Rio de Janeiro, Brazil; Maria Emilia Rey Silva, **UCBEU,** São Paulo, Brazil; Carmen Moreno, **IMPACT Institute,** Las Condes, Chile; Liliana Baltra, **Instituto Chileno Norteamericano,** Santiago de Chile; Amnerys Barrientos Usman, **Corporación Universitaria Tecnológica de Bolívar,** Cartagena, Colombia; Paul Dean Warman, **Tokyo Air Travel College,** Tokyo, Japan; Claude Arnaud and Paul Chris McVay, **Toyo Women's College,** Tokyo, Japan; Michael Barnes, **Tokyu Be Seminar,** Japan; Valerie Benson, **Suzugamine Women's College,** Hiroshima, Japan; Eric Bray, **Kyoto YMCA English School,** Kyoto, Japan; James Hale, **Sundai ELS,** Japan; Christopher Lynch, **Sunshine College,** Tokyo, Japan; Mike Millin and Kelley Seymour, **James English School,** Japan; John Pak, **Yokohama YMCA English School,** Yokohama, Japan; Lynne Roecklein, **Gifu University,** Japan; Hae-Kyong Park, **Handong University,** Pohang, Korea; Mae-Ran Park, **Pukyong National University,** Pusan, Korea; Luís Hernández Acosta, **Instituto Mexicano Norteamericano de Relaciones Culturales (IMARC),** Saltillo, Mexico; Matilde Legorreta and Manuel Hidalgo, **Kratos, S.A. de C.V.,** Mexico D.F.; Lilia Ortega Sepúlveda, **Unidad Lomoa Hermosa,** Mexico D.F.; Elizabeth Restivo, **St. Augustine College,** Chicago, Illinois, USA; Kim Sanabria, **Columbia University,** New York, New York, USA; Peg Donner, Ricia Doren, and Andrew Sachar, **Rancho Santiago College Centennial Education Center,** Santa Ana, California, USA; and the many teachers around the world who responded to the *Interchange* questionnaire.

The **editorial** and **production** team:

Sylvia P. Bloch, John Borrelli, Liane Carita, Mary Carson, Karen Davy, Randee Falk, Andrew Gitzy, Christa Hansen, Pauline Ireland, Stephanie Karras, Penny Laporte, Sharon Lee, Tay Lesley, José Antonio Méndez, James R. Morgan, Kathy Niemczyk, Linda Olle, Kathleen O'Reilly, Howard Siegelman, Jane Sturtevant, and Mary Vaughn.

And Cambridge University Press **staff** and **advisors**:

Carlos Barbisan, Natalia Bochorishvili, Kathleen Corley, Kate Cory-Wright, Riitta da Costa, Peter Davison, Peter Donovan, Robert Gallo, Cecilia Gómez, Bob Hands, Colin Hayes, Catherine Higham, James Hursthouse, Koen Van Landeghem, Alejandro Martínez, Nigel McQuitty, Carine Mitchell, Lu-Ann Ong, Chuanpit Phalavadhana, Andrew Robinson, Dan Schulte, Cathy Smith, Ian Sutherland, Janaka Williams, and Ellen Zlotnick.

Plan of the Book

Title/Topics	Functions	Grammar
UNIT 1 — PAGES 2–7		
It's nice to meet you. Alphabet; greetings and leave-takings; names and titles of address; numbers 1–10 and telephone numbers	Introducing yourself and friends; saying hello and good-bye; asking for names and phone numbers	Possessive adjectives *my, your, his, her*; the verb *be*: affirmative statements and contractions
UNIT 2 — PAGES 8–13		
What's this? Possessions, classroom objects, personal items, and locations in a room	Naming objects; asking for and giving the location of an object	Articles *a, an,* and *the*; *this/it* and *these/they*; plurals; yes/no and *where* questions with *be*; prepositions of place
UNIT 3 — PAGES 14–19		
Where are you from? Cities, countries, and regions; adjectives of personality; numbers to 100 and age	Talking about geographical locations; asking for and giving information about places of origin, nationality, native language, and age; describing people	The verb *be*: affirmative and negative statements, yes/no questions, short answers, and Wh-questions
UNIT 4 — PAGES 20–25		
I'm not wearing boots! Clothing; colors; seasons of the year; weather	Asking about and describing clothing; talking about the weather; finding the owner of an item	Possessive adjectives *our, their,* and possessives of names; present continuous affirmative and negative statements; *isn't* and *aren't*; conjunctions *and* and *but*; color adjectives before nouns
REVIEW OF UNITS 1–4 — PAGES 26–27		
UNIT 5 — PAGES 28–33		
What are you doing? Times of the day, clock time; daily activities, Saturday activities	Asking for and telling time; asking about and describing current activities	Questions with *what time*; *what* + *doing* and Wh-questions with the present continuous; conjunction *so*
UNIT 6 — PAGES 34–39		
We live in the suburbs. Places and transportation; family relationships; daily routines; days of the week	Asking for and giving information about where people live and how they go to work or school; talking about family members; talking about daily routines	Simple present statements with regular and irregular verbs; simple present yes/no and Wh-questions; time expressions
UNIT 7 — PAGES 40–45		
Does the apartment have a view? Houses and apartments; rooms; furniture	Asking about and describing homes; saying what furniture is in a room	Simple present short answers; *how many*; *there is, there are*; *there's no, there isn't a, there are no, there aren't any*
UNIT 8 — PAGES 46–51		
What do you do? Occupations and workplaces	Asking for and giving information about work; giving opinions about jobs	Simple present Wh-questions with *do*; placement of adjectives before nouns; descriptive adjectives for occupations
REVIEW OF UNITS 5–8 — PAGES 52–53		

Listening/Pronunciation	Writing/Reading	Interchange Activity
Listening for the spelling of names; listening for telephone numbers Pronunciation of the alphabet and numbers 1–10	Writing a list of telephone numbers	"Directory assistance": Calling the operator to find out phone numbers
Listening to find the location of an item Pronunciation of plural s	Writing the location of objects	"Find the differences": Comparing two rooms
Listening for countries and languages; listening to descriptions of people Syllabic stress of numbers; blending with is and are	Writing questions requesting personal information	"Class personalities": Identifying classmates' personality traits
Listening for descriptions of clothing Sentence stress and rhythm	Writing questions about what people are wearing	"Celebrity fashions": Describing celebrities' clothing
Listening for the time; listening to identify what people are doing Question intonation	Writing about what people are doing "It's Saturday! What Are You Doing?": Reading about Saturday activities	"Time zones": Talking about what people are doing in different cities around the world
Listening to people describe how they go to work or school; listening for days of the week Pronunciation of third-person singular s	Writing about daily schedules and habits "What's Your Schedule Like?": Reading about daily schedules	"Class survey": Finding out more about classmates' daily schedules and habits
Listening to descriptions of houses and apartments; listening to people shop for furniture Pronunciation of th	Writing about a dream house "Two Special Houses in the American Southwest": Reading about unique houses	"Find the differences": Comparing two apartments
Listening to people describe their jobs Reduction of do and does	Writing about jobs "What Do You Do, Exactly?": Reading about people's occupations	"The perfect job": Figuring out what job is right for you

Title/Topics	Functions/Vocabulary	Grammar
UNIT 9 PAGES 54–59		
Broccoli is good for you. Food Pyramid: basic foods; desserts; meals	Talking about foods that are good or bad for you, food likes and dislikes, and eating habits; talking about food items you need	Countable and uncountable nouns; *some* and *any*; adverbs of frequency: *always, usually, often, sometimes, seldom, never*
UNIT 10 PAGES 60–65		
You can play baseball really well. Sports; talents and abilities	Talking about sports you like and dislike; talking about talents and abilities	Simple present Wh-questions; *can* for ability
UNIT 11 PAGES 66–71		
What are you going to do? Months and dates; birthdays, holidays, and celebrations	Saying dates; asking about birthdays; asking for and giving information about future plans, holidays, and celebrations	The future with *be going to*: Wh-questions with *be going to*; future time expressions
UNIT 12 PAGES 72–77		
What's the matter? Parts of the body; health problems and advice; medications	Talking about illnesses and health problems; giving advice; giving instructions	*Have* + noun; *feel* + adjective; affirmative and negative imperatives
REVIEW OF UNITS 9–12 PAGES 78–79		
UNIT 13 PAGES 80–85		
You can't miss it. Stores and things you can buy; locations in a city; tourist attractions	Talking about shopping; asking for and giving locations and directions	Prepositions of place: *on, on the corner of, across from, next to, between*; giving directions with imperatives
UNIT 14 PAGES 86–91		
Did you have a good weekend? Weekends: household chores and leisure activities	Asking for and giving information about activities in the recent past	Simple past statements with regular and irregular verbs; simple past yes/no questions and short answers
UNIT 15 PAGES 92–97		
Where were you born? Biographical information; years; school subjects	Asking for and giving information about date and place of birth, school experiences, and the recent past	Statements and questions with the past of *be*; Wh-questions with *did, was,* and *were*
UNIT 16 PAGES 98–103		
Please leave us a message. Telephone calls and invitations; going out with friends	Making phone calls; leaving phone messages; inviting people and accepting and declining invitations; making excuses	Object pronouns; verb + *to* + verb; *would*
REVIEW OF UNITS 13–16 PAGES 104–105		
UNIT SUMMARIES PAGES S-2–S-17		
APPENDIX		

1 It's nice to meet you.

1 CONVERSATION

A Listen and practice.

Michael: Hi. My name is Michael Parker.
Jennifer: I'm Jennifer Yang.
Michael: It's nice to meet you, Jennifer.
Jennifer: Nice to meet you, too.
Michael: I'm sorry. What's your last name again?
Jennifer: It's Yang.

B *Pair work* Introduce yourself to your partner.

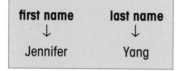

first name	last name
↓	↓
Jennifer	Yang

2 SNAPSHOT

 Listen and practice.

Popular First Names in the United States

for males		for females	
Christopher	Joshua	Ashley	Lisa
David	Matthew	Jennifer	Michelle
James *santiago*	Michael	Jessica	Nicole
Jason	Robert	Katherine	Sarah
John	Steven	Kimberly	Stephanie

Source: *The Cambridge Encyclopedia*, Third Edition

What is another first name for a male in English?
  for a female?
What is your favorite first name in English?
List some popular names in your country.

2

3 GRAMMAR FOCUS

My, your, his, her

What's **your** name?

My name is Jennifer.

What's **his** name?

His name is Michael.

What's **her** name?

Her name is Nicole.

What's = What is

Group work Play "The Name Game." Make a circle.
Learn the names of your classmates.

A: My name is Keiko.
B: Her name is Keiko. I'm Akira.
C: Her name is Keiko. His name is Akira. And I'm Kumiko.

4 WORD POWER *The alphabet*

A Listen and practice.

A B C D E F G H I J K L M N O P Q R S T U V W X Y Z
a b c d e f g h i j k l m n o p q r s t u v w x y z

B Group work Listen. Then practice using your
own information. Write down your classmates' names.

A: What's your name?
B: I'm Sarah Conner.
A: Is that S-A-R-A-H?
B: Yes, that's right.
A: How do you spell your last name? C-O-N-N-O-R?
B: No, it's C-O-N-N-E-R.

Students in my class
Sarah Conner
Jennifer Yang

5 LISTENING *Spelling names*

How do you spell the names? Listen
and check (✓) the correct answers.

1. ☑ Jon   ☐ John
2. ☐ Sara   ☐ Sarah
3. ☐ Steven   ☐ Stephen
4. ☐ Katherine ☐ Kathryn
5. ☐ Kris   ☐ Chris

6 SAYING HELLO

A 🔊 Listen and practice.

1

Hi, Matthew. How are you?

Great! How about you, Lisa?

2

Good morning, Mr. Duran. How are you?

I'm just fine, Alex. Thank you.

3

Good afternoon, Brad. How are you?

Not bad, thanks. How are you?

4

Good evening, Mrs. Morgan.

Hello, Ms. Chen. How are you?

I'm OK, thank you.

TITLES		
For males: Mr.	**For females:** Ms. Miss Mrs.	**Use titles with older people:** Good morning, Mr. Duran. **Use titles to show respect:** Good evening, Mrs. Morgan.

B *Class activity* Go around the class. Practice greeting your classmates formally (with titles) and informally (without titles).

7 CONVERSATION

A Listen and practice.

Jennifer: Excuse me. Are you
            Steven Carson?
David: No, I'm not. He's over there.
Jennifer: Oh, I'm sorry. *Contracciones*

Jennifer: Steven? This is your book.
Steven: Oh, it's my math book! Thanks.
        You're in my class, right?
Jennifer: Yes, I am. I'm Jennifer Yang.
Steven: It's nice to meet you.

Steven: David, this is Jennifer.
       She's in our math class.
David: Hi, Jennifer.
Jennifer: Hi, David. Nice to meet you.

B *Group work* Greet a classmate.
Then introduce him or her to another
classmate.

8 GRAMMAR FOCUS

CLASS AUDIO ONLY ▶

The verb be 🔊

I'm Jennifer Yang.	**Are you** Steven Carson?	**I'm** = I am
You're in my class.	Yes, **I am.**	**You're** = You are
She's in our math class. (**Jennifer is** in our math class.)	No, **I'm not.**	**He's** = He is
He's over there. (**Steven is** over there.)		**She's** = She is
It's my math book.	How **are you?**	**It's** = It is
It's Yang. (**My last name is** Yang.)	**I'm** fine.	

A Complete the conversation with the correct words in parentheses.
Then practice with a partner.

David: Hello, Jennifer. How ....*are*.... you? (is/are)
Jennifer: *I'm*........ fine, thanks. (She's/I'm)
       I'm..... sorry – what's your name again? (I'm/It's)
David: *It's*...... David – David Medina. (He's/It's)
Jennifer: That's right! David, this ...*is*...... Sarah Conner. (is/am)
      She's..... in our math class. (She's/He's)
David: Hi, Sarah. ..*It's*.... nice to meet you. (I'm/It's)
Sarah: Hi, David. I think *you're*.. in my English class, too. (you're/I'm)
David: Oh, right! Yes, I ..*am*.... . (are/am)

B Complete the conversation. Then practice in groups.

Nicole: Excuse me. .....*Are*..... you Steven Carson?
David: No, ...I'm..... not. My name .....is.....
David Medina. Steven .....is..... over there.
Nicole: Oh, sorry.

Nicole: .....are..... you Steven Carson?
Steven: Yes, I .....am..... .
Nicole: Hi. .....I'm..... Nicole Johnson.
Steven: Oh, ...you are.....in my math class, right?
Nicole: Yes, I .....am...... .
Steven: .....It's..... nice to meet you.

C *Class activity* Write your name on a piece of paper. Put the papers in a pile. Take a paper from the pile. Find the other student.

A: Excuse me. Are you Sonia Gomes?
B: No, I'm not.

A: Hi. Are you Sonia Gomes?
C: Yes, I am.

---

9 NUMBERS

A 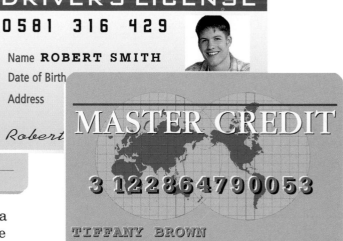 Listen and practice.

0	1	2	3	4	5	6	7	8	9	10
zero (oh)	one	two	three	four	five	six	seven	eight	nine	ten

B Say these numbers.

NEW AGE HEALTH CLUB
Name: **Michelle Jenkins**
Membership #: **38342**

DRIVER'S LICENSE
0581 316 429
Name **ROBERT SMITH**
Date of Birth
Address
Robert

MASTER CREDIT
3 122864790053
TIFFANY BROWN

C 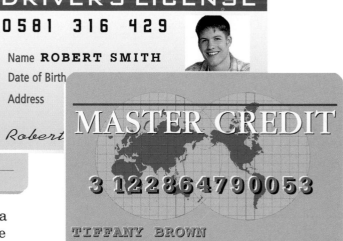 *Group work* Listen. Then make a list of names and phone numbers for people in your group.

A: What's your name?
B: I'm Michelle Jenkins.
A: And what's your phone number?
B: It's 555-2491.

10 LISTENING

Jennifer and Michael are making a list of telephone numbers of classmates. Listen and complete the information.

☎	
Name	Telephone number
David Medina	555-1937
Sarah Conner	
James Sato	
Anna Silva	
Steven Carson	
Nicole Johnson	
Jennifer Yang	
Michael Parker	

interchange 1

Directory assistance
Call for some phone numbers. Student A turns to page IC-2. Student B turns to page IC-4.

11 SAYING GOOD-BYE

A Listen and practice.

B *Class activity* Go around the room. Practice saying good-bye to your classmates and to your teacher.

What's this?

1 SNAPSHOT

Listen and practice.

On-Line Shopping

pager

CD player

sunglasses

watch

calculator

camera

cell phone

electronic address book

Check (✓) the things you have.
Choose two things you want.

2 ARTICLES *Classroom objects*

A Listen. Complete these sentences with **a** or **an**.

Articles
an + vowel sound
a + consonant sound

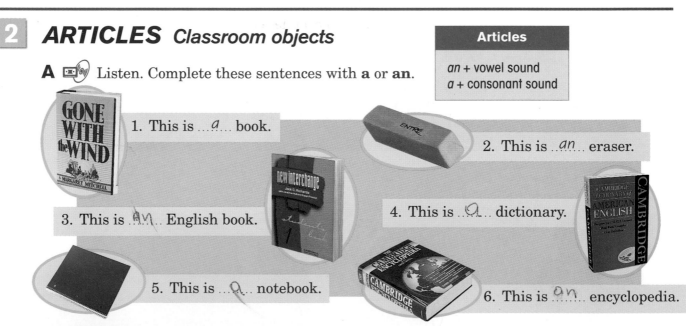

1. This is ...*a*... book.

2. This is ..*an*.. eraser.

3. This is ..*an*.. English book.

4. This is ...*a*... dictionary.

5. This is ...*a*... notebook.

6. This is ..*an*.. encyclopedia.

B *Pair work* Find these things in your classroom.

wastebasket	pen	desk	map	table
English dictionary	pencil	book bag	board	window
cassette player	clock	chair	wall	door

A: This is a wastebasket.
B: How do you spell *wastebasket*?
A: W-A-S-T-E-B-A-S-K-E-T.

8

3 CONVERSATION

 Listen and practice.

Wendy: Wow! What's this?
 Helen: It's a camera.
Wendy: Oh, cool! Thank you, Helen.
        It's great!
 Helen: You're welcome.
   Rex: Now open this box!
Wendy: OK. Uh, what are these?
   Rex: They're earrings.
Wendy: Oh. They're . . . interesting.
        Thank you, Rex. They're very nice.

4 PRONUNCIATION *Plural* s

A Listen and practice. Notice the pronunciation of the plural **s** endings.

s = /z/		s = /s/		(e)s = /ɪz/	
telephone	telephones	desk	desks	sentence	sentences
camera	cameras	map	maps	exercise	exercises
book bag	book bags	wastebasket	wastebaskets	watch	watches

B Say the plural forms of these nouns. Then complete the chart.

newspaper   briefcase   clock   key   address

purse   stamp   television   wallet

/z/	/s/	/ɪz/
newspapers		

C Listen and check your answers.

5 GRAMMAR FOCUS

This/It, these/they; *plurals*

This is a camera.

These are cameras.

What**'s this?** **It's an** earring.

What **are these?** **They're** earrings.

It's = It is
They're = They are

Complete these conversations. Then practice with a partner.

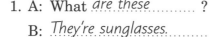

1. A: What <u>are these</u> ?
   B: <u>They're sunglasses.</u>

2. A: What <u>'s this</u> ?
   B: <u>It's a watch.</u>

3. A: What .... ?
   B: ....

4. A: What .... ?
   B: ....

5. A: What .... ?
   B: ....

6. A: What .... ?
   B: ....

6 WHAT'S THIS CALLED?

A Listen and practice.

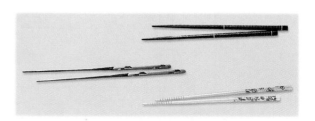

A: What's this called in English?
B: I don't know.
C: It's an umbrella.
A: How do you spell that?
C: U-M-B-R-E-L-L-A.

A: What are these called in English?
B: Hmm. I think they're chopsticks.
A: How do you spell that?
B: C-H-O-P-S-T-I-C-K-S.

B *Group work* Choose four things. Put them in the center of the group. Take turns asking about the name and spelling of each thing.

7 CONVERSATION

 Listen and practice.

Kate: Oh, no! Where are my car keys?
Joe: Relax, Kate. Are they in your purse?
Kate: No, they're not. They're gone!
Joe: I bet they're still on the table in the restaurant.
Waiter: Excuse me. Are these your keys?
Kate: Yes, they are. Thank you!
Joe: See? No problem.
Waiter: And is this your wallet?
Kate: Hmm. No, it's not. Where is your wallet, Joe?
Joe: In my pocket. . . . Wait a minute! That's my wallet!

The CORNER RESTAURANT

8 GRAMMAR FOCUS

Yes/No and where questions with be

Is this your wallet?	**Are your keys** in your purse?
Yes, **it is**.	Yes, **they are**.
No, **it's not**.	No, **they're not**.
Where is your wallet?	**Where are my keys?**
It's in my pocket.	They're in the restaurant.

A Complete these conversations. Then practice them.

1. A: Where ....*are*.... my glasses?

   B: Are .*they*. in your bag?

   A: No, they're .*not*. .

   B: Wait! ....*Are*.. they in your pocket?

   A: Yes, ...*they* are. Thanks!

2. A: ....*is*.... this my pen?

   B: No, .*it's*.. not. It's *my* pen.

   A: Sorry. .*where*. is my pen?

   B: .*It's*. on your desk.

   A: Yes, it ....*is*.... . You're right!

B *Group work* Put three things from the classroom, your pocket, or your bag in a box. Find the owner of each item.

A: Is this your pen, Young-ho?
B: No, it's not.

A: Is this your pen, Sun-hee?
C: Let me see. Yes, it is.

9 WORD POWER *Prepositions; article* the

A Listen and practice.

Where are **the** keys? **The** keys are in **the** briefcase.

in in front of behind

on next to under

B Complete these sentences. Listen and check your answers.

1. The books are *in the book bag* .

2. The CD player is *next to TV* .

3. The map is *under the new paper* .

4. The chair is *behind the desk*

5. The wallet is *on the purse* .

6. The phone is ....

C *Pair work* Now ask and answer questions about the photos in part B.

A: Where are the books?
B: They're in the book bag.

10 LISTENING

  Kate is looking for some things in her house.
Where are they? Listen and match each thing to its location.

1. earrings   a. under the table
2. watch   b. on the chair
3. sunglasses   c. in front of the television
4. address book   d. in her purse

11 WHERE ARE MY THINGS?

Pair work Joe is looking for these things. Ask and answer questions.

pager	glasses
briefcase	umbrella
keys	cell phone
wallet	notebook

A: Where is his pager?
B: It's in front of the television.

interchange 2

Find the differences

Compare two pictures of a room. Turn to page IC-3.

3 Where are you from?

1 SNAPSHOT

 Listen and practice.

THE TEN LARGEST CITIES IN THE WORLD (Based on the population of the metropolitan area)	CITIES	COUNTRIES
	1. Tokyo 2. Mexico City 3. São Paulo 4. New York 5. Bombay 6. Shanghai 7. Los Angeles 8. Calcutta 9. Buenos Aires 10. Seoul	Argentina Brazil China India Japan Mexico South Korea The United States

Source: http://www.infoplease.com

Where are these cities? Match the cities to the countries. Check your answers in the appendix.
What are some large cities in your country?

2 CONVERSATION Examen

A Listen and practice.

Tim: Where are you from, Jessica?
Jessica: Well, my family is here in the United States, but we're from Korea originally.
Tim: Oh, my mother is Korean – from Seoul! Are you from Seoul?
Jessica: No, we're not from Seoul. We're from Pusan.
Tim: So is your first language Korean? [ian]
Jessica: Yes, it is. [First]

B Listen to Jessica and Tim talk to Tony, Natasha, and Monique. Check (✓) **True** or **False**.

CLASS
AUDIO
ONLY

	True	False
1. Tony is from Italy.	☐	☐
2. Natasha is from New York.	☐	☐
3. Monique's first language is English.	☐	☐

3 GRAMMAR FOCUS

Statements and yes/no questions with be 🔊

Are you from Seoul?	**I'm not** from Seoul.	**I'm** from Pusan.
Is Tony from Italy?	**He's not** from Italy.	**He's** from Brazil.
Is your first language French?	**It's not** French.	**It's** English.
Are you and Maria from Chile?	**We're not** from Chile.	**We're** from Argentina.
Are your parents in the U.S.?	**They're not** in the U.S.	**They're** in Europe.

Are your parents in the U.S.?　　Are you and your family from Asia?
Yes, they are.　　**Yes, we are.**
No, they're not.　　**No, we're not.**　　we're = we are

For a list of countries, nationalities, and languages, see the appendix.

Kyoto
London
São Paulo

A Complete the conversations. Then practice with a partner.

1. A: Hiroshi, ...*are*..... you and Maiko from Japan?
   B: Yes, we ...*are*....
   A: ..*are*.. you from Tokyo?
   B: No, *I'm* not. *I'm* from Kyoto.

2. A: ....*is*.. Laura from the U.S.?
   B: No, *she's* not. She's from the U.K.
   A: ...*is*..... she from London?
   B: Yes, she ....*is*.... . But her parents ...*are*... from Italy originally.
   A: ....*is*..... Italian her first language?
   B: No, *it's* not. ...*is*..... English.

3. A: ..*are*.. Elena and Carlos from Mexico?
   B: No, *they're* not. ..*are*.. from Peru.
   A: What about you? Where ...*are*... you from?
   B: *I'm* from São Paulo.
   A: So your first language ....*is*... Portuguese.
   B: Yes, it ...*is*..... .

B Match the questions with the answers.
Then practice with a partner.

1. Are you and your family from Canada? ..*d*.. 　a. No, he's not. He's from Singapore.
2. Is your first language English? ...... 　b. Yes, she is. She's from California.
3. Are you Brazilian? ..*e*.. 　c. No, it's not. My first language is Japanese.
4. Is Mr. Ho from Hong Kong? ...... 　d. No, we're not. We're from Australia.
5. Is your mother from the United States? ...... 　e. Yes, we are. We're from São Paulo.

C *Pair work* Write five questions like the ones in part B.
Ask and answer your questions with a partner.

4 REGIONS OF THE WORLD

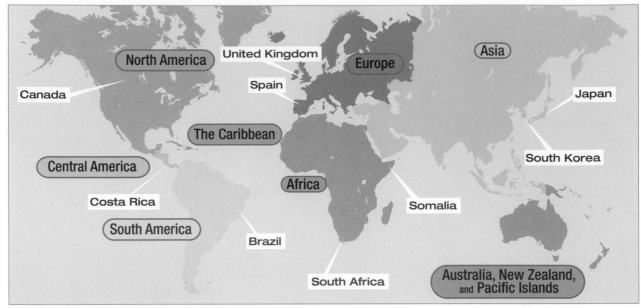

North America
United Kingdom
Europe
Asia
Canada
Spain
Japan
The Caribbean
South Korea
Central America
Africa
Costa Rica
Somalia
South America
Brazil
South Africa
Australia, New Zealand, and Pacific Islands

See the appendix for a list of countries and nationalities.

A *Group work* Name two more countries in each of these regions. Compare your charts.

Europe	Africa	Asia	South America	North America
....	....	....	....	....
....	....	....	....	....

A: France is in Europe.
B: Greece is in Europe, too.

B *Pair work* Where are these people from?

Antonio Banderas   Yuka Honda   Nelson Mandela   Celine Dion   Pelé   Se Ri Pak

Student A: Guess where these people are from. Ask Student B questions.

Student B: Turn to the appendix. Use the map to answer Student A's questions.

A: Is Antonio Banderas from Puerto Rico?
B: No, he's not.
A: Is he from Spain?
B: Yes, he is. That's right.

5 CONVERSATION

Listen and practice.

Emma: Who's that?
  Jill: He's my brother. *quiut*
Emma: Wow! He's cute. What's his name?
  Jill: James. We call him Jim. He's in
      college here in Vancouver. *VANCUUVER*
Emma: Oh, how old is he?
  Jill: He's twenty-one years old.
Emma: What's he like? I bet he's nice.
  Jill: Yes, he is – and he's very funny, too!

6 NUMBERS AND AGES

A Listen and practice.

11 eleven	**21** twenty-one	**40** forty
12 twelve	**22** twenty-two	**50** fifty
13 thirteen	**23** twenty-three	**60** sixty
14 fourteen	**24** twenty-four	**70** seventy
15 fifteen	**25** twenty-five	**80** eighty
16 sixteen	**26** twenty-six	**90** ninety
17 seventeen	**27** twenty-seven	**100** one hundred
18 eighteen	**28** twenty-eight	**101** one hundred and one
19 nineteen	**29** twenty-nine	**102** one hundred and two
20 twenty	**30** thirty	

B Listen and practice. Notice the pronunciation.

thirtéen – thírty   fourtéen – fórty   fiftéen – fífty   sixtéen – síxty

C *Group work* How old are the people on page 16? Write down your guesses
and then compare. (Check your answers on page S-4 in the Unit Summaries.)

A: How old is Antonio Banderas?
B: I think he's twenty-nine (years old).
C: I think he's thirty-five. . . .

7 WORD POWER Descriptions

A Listen and practice.

She's pretty.

He's serious.

She's smart.

He's handsome.

She's shy.

They're very good-looking.

He's very funny.

She's really friendly.

They're nice.

He's really tall.

He's thin.

He's short.

He's a little heavy.

B Complete the chart with words from part A. Add two more words to each list.

Appearance		Personality	
heavy	....	friendly	....
....	....	....	....
....	....	....	....

8 LISTENING

 CLASS AUDIO ONLY

 Listen to descriptions of four people. Check (✓) the correct words.

Descriptions			
1. Karen	☑ friendly	☑ short	☐ tall
2. James	☐ funny	☐ nice	☐ thin
3. Stephanie	☐ cute	☐ shy	☐ smart
4. Andrew	☐ a little heavy	☐ handsome	☐ funny

interchange 3

Class personalities

What are people in your class like? Turn to page IC-5.

9 PRONUNCIATION *Blending with* is *and* are

🔊 Listen and practice. Notice how **is** and **are** blend with Wh-question words.

Who's that? **What's** he like? **Who are** they? **What are** they like?

10 GRAMMAR FOCUS

Wh-questions with be 🔊

What's your name?	**Who's that?**	**Who are they?**	**Who's = Who is**
My name is Jill.	He's my brother.	They're my classmates.	
Where are you from?	**How old is he?**	**Where are they from?**	
I'm from Canada.	He's twenty-one.	They're from Rio de Janeiro.	
How are you today?	**What's he like?**	**What's Rio like?**	
I'm just fine.	He's very funny.	It's very beautiful.	

A Complete the conversations with Wh-questions. Then practice with a partner.

1. A: Look! ......*Who's that*...... ?
   B: Oh – he's a new student.
   A: .... ?
   B: I think his name is Chien Kuo.
   A: Chien Kuo? .... ?
   B: He's from China.

2. A: Keiko, ... ?
   B: I'm from Japan – from Kyoto.
   A: .... ?
   B: Kyoto is very old and beautiful.
   A: By the way, ... ?
   B: It's Noguchi. N-O-G-U-C-H-I.

3. A: Hi, John. .... ?
   B: I'm just fine. My friend Carolina is here this week – from Argentina.
   A: Carolina? I don't know her.
   .... ?
   B: She's really pretty and very smart.
   A: .... ?
   B: She's eighteen years old.

B *Pair work* Write five Wh-questions about your partner and five questions about your partner's best friend. Take turns asking and answering questions.

Your partner	Your partner's best friend
Where are you from?	Who's your best friend?

4 I'm not wearing boots!

1 WORD POWER Clothes

A Listen and practice.

Clothes for Work

shirt
tie
belt
jacket }
pants } suit
coat
shoes

blouse
scarf
skirt
(high) heels

raincoat
dress

Clothes for Leisure

hat
cap
T-shirt
sweater
jeans
shorts
gloves
socks
sneakers
boots

pajamas
swimsuits

B *Pair work* Fill in the chart with words from part A. Add two more words to each list. Then compare answers with your partner.

Clothes for warm weather	Clothes for cold weather
....	....
....	....
....	....
....	....
....	....

20

2 COLORS

A 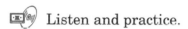 Listen and practice.

white	light gray	gray
dark gray	beige	light brown
brown	dark brown	black

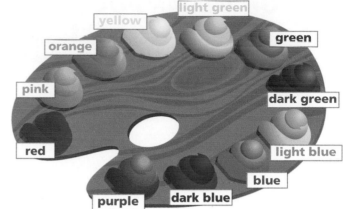

yellow · light green · orange · green · pink · dark green · red · light blue · blue · purple · dark blue

B *Group work* Ask about favorite colors.

A: What are your favorite colors?
B: My favorite colors are red and purple.

C *Group work* Describe the clothes in Exercise 1.

A: The suit is blue.
B: The T-shirt is light green.

3 CONVERSATION

Listen and practice.

Pat: Are our clothes dry?
Julie: Yes, they are.
Pat: Where are my favorite socks?
Julie: What color are they?
Pat: They're white.
Julie: Are these your socks?
They're blue and white.
Pat: No, they're probably Liz's socks. Wait! They *are* my socks! They're ruined!
Julie: Yeah. The problem is this T-shirt. It's dark blue.
Pat: Is it Liz's?
Julie: Actually, it's *my* T-shirt. I'm sorry.
Pat: That's OK. It's not important.

4 PRONUNCIATION *Sentence stress and rhythm*

Listen and practice. Notice the stress in these sentences.

A: What **cól**or is Julie's **T**-shirt?
B: It's **dárk blúe**.

A: What **cól**or are Pat's **sócks**?
B: They're **blúe** and **white**.

5 GRAMMAR FOCUS

cosas pertenece a l
con posesivos
Examen

Possessives

					Pronunciation	
Are **our** clothes dry?	Are **Julie's** and **Pat's** clothes OK?	I → my			Pat's	/s/
Where are **my** socks?	No, **their** clothes aren't OK.	you → your			Julie's	/z/
Are these **your** socks?	What's **Josh's** favorite color?	he → his			Liz's	/ɪz/
Is this **Liz's** T-shirt?	**His** favorite color is blue.	she → her				
No, it's not **her** T-shirt.		we → our				
		they → their				

A Write a question for each sentence. Compare with a partner. Then ask and answer the questions.

1. Liz's jeans are black.   What color *are Liz's jeans* ?
2. Dan's favorite color is green.   What .... ?
3. James's shoes are on the table!   Where .... ?
4. Julie's T-shirt is dark blue.   What color .... ?
5. Debbie and Jeff's house is white.   What color .... ?
6. My favorite color is purple.   What .... ?
7. Our classroom is light yellow.   What color .... ?

A: What color are Liz's jeans?
B: Her jeans are black.

> Go to page ii of the Video Activity Book for a
> supplementary lesson on possessive pronouns.

B *Group work* Write five questions about your classmates.
Ask and answer your questions.

A: What color is Maria's skirt?   B: What color are Victor's shoes?
B: Her skirt is . . . .   C: His shoes are . . . .

6 LISTENING

A Listen to these people describe their clothes. Number the
pictures from 1 to 4.

B *Pair work* Now talk
about these people. What
colors are their clothes?

A: What color is Peter's
   T-shirt?
B: His T-shirt is yellow.

Bob	Elizabeth	Diane	1	Peter

7 SNAPSHOT

 Listen and practice.

Weather in the United States and Canada

IT'S WINTER. . . .
It's snowing. It's very cold.

IT'S SPRING. . . .
It's raining. It's warm.

IT'S SUMMER. . . .
It's very sunny, hot, and humid.

IT'S FALL. . . .
It's cool. It's cloudy and windy.

What's the weather like in your city today?
What are the seasons in your country? Are they the same as in the U.S. and Canada?
What season is it now?
What's your favorite season?

8 CONVERSATION

 Listen and practice.

Pat: Uh-oh!
Julie: What's the matter?
Pat: It's snowing, and it's very cold!
Julie: Are you wearing a scarf?
Pat: No, I'm not.
Julie: Well, you're wearing a coat.
Pat: But I'm not wearing boots!
Julie: OK. Let's take a taxi.
Pat: Thanks, Julie.

9 GRAMMAR FOCUS

Present continuous statements; isn't and aren't 🔊

I'm	I'm not	OR:	Conjunctions
You're	You aren't	You're not	It's snowing,
She's wearing shoes.	She isn't wearing boots.	She's not	**and** it's very cold.
We're	We aren't	We're not	I'm wearing a coat,
They're	They aren't	They're not	**but** I'm not wearing boots.
It's snowing.	It isn't raining.	It's not	

A Complete these sentences. Then compare with a partner.

1. My name's Claire. I 'm wearing a black suit today. I 'm wearing high heels, too. It's raining, but I 'm not wearing a raincoat.

2. It's hot today. Dan and Sally are wearing shorts and T-shirts. It's very sunny, but they aren't wearing sunglasses.

3. Phil is wearing a suit today – he is wearing pants and a jacket. He is wearing a white shirt, but he isn't wearing a tie.

4. It's cold today, but Kathy is not wearing a coat. She is wearing a sweatshirt, gloves, and a hat. She is not wearing boots. She is wearing running shoes.

Present continuous yes/no questions

			adjective + noun
Are you **wearing** a black suit?	Yes, I **am**.	No, I**'m not**.	My sult Is black.
Is she **wearing** boots?	Yes, she **is**.	No, she**'s not**. No, she **isn't**.	I'm wearing **a black suit**.
Are they **wearing** sunglasses?	Yes, they **are**.	No, they**'re not**. No, they **aren't**.	

B *Pair work* Ask and answer the questions about the pictures in part A.

1. Is Claire wearing a black suit?
2. Is she wearing a raincoat?
3. Is she wearing high heels?
4. Is Phil wearing gray pants?
5. Is he wearing a white shirt?
6. Is he wearing a tie?

7. Are Dan and Sally wearing swimsuits?
8. Are they wearing shorts?
9. Are they wearing sunglasses?
10. Is Kathy wearing boots?
11. Is she wearing a coat?
12. Is she wearing a hat and gloves?

A: Is Claire wearing a black suit?
B: Yes, she is.
A: Is she wearing a raincoat?
B: No, she isn't. (No, she's not.)

C *Pair work* Write four more questions about the pictures in part A. Ask and answer questions with your partner.

10 LISTENING

CLASS
AUDIO
ONLY

A 🔊 Listen. Write the names
Bruce, Beth, Jon, Anita, and **Nick**
in the correct boxes.

B *Pair work* Talk about the people
in the picture.

A: Jon is wearing a white T-shirt.
B: And he's wearing blue pants.

C *Group work* Write questions
about six people in your class. Then
take turns asking and answering
the questions.

> *Are Sonia and Paulo wearing jeans?*
> *Is Paulo wearing a red shirt?*

Jon

interchange 4

Celebrity fashions
What are your favorite
celebrities wearing?
Turn to pages IC-6
and IC-7.

Review of Units 1-4

Examen

1 WHAT'S THE QUESTION?

Pair work Match the questions with the answers and practice with a partner.
Then take turns asking the questions. Answer with your own information.

1. What's your name? ...d...
2. Where are you and your family from? ...C...
3. How are you today? ...K...
4. What color are your shoes? ...F...
5. What's your favorite color? ...h...
6. What's your telephone number? ...b...
7. Who is your best friend? ...a...
8. What's your best friend like? ...J...
9. How old is he? ...l...
10. Where's my English book? ...e...
11. What's our teacher wearing today? ...g...
12. How do you spell *calculator*? ...i...

a. My best friend is Ken.
b. It's 555-3493.
c. We're from Thailand.
d. My name is Sarah Smith.
e. It's under your chair.
f. They're black.
g. He's wearing a suit and tie.
h. It's purple.
i. It's C-A-L-C-U-L-A-T-O-R.
j. He's funny and very smart.
k. I'm just great!
l. He's sixteen years old.

2 LISTENING

CLASS AUDIO ONLY

A Listen to the conversations. Complete the chart.

 1

 2

 3

 4

Who are they?	Where are they from?
1. *Ryan*	
2.	
3.	
4.	

B ***Pair work*** Write five questions about these people.
Then take turns asking and answering your questions.

A: Is Ryan very tall?
B: No, he's not. . . .

3 WHAT'S WRONG?

What's wrong with this room?
Write down five problems.
Then compare with a partner.

The umbrella is behind the picture.

4 SAME OR DIFFERENT?

Pair work Choose two classmates. Are their clothes the same or different? Write five sentences. Then compare with a partner.

Same
Jun and Akira are both wearing blue jeans.
Different
Jun is wearing boots, but Akira is wearing shoes.

5 What are you doing?

1 CONVERSATION

Listen and practice.

Debbie: Hello?
John: Hi, Debbie. This is John.
I'm calling from Australia.
Debbie: Australia?
John: I'm at a conference in Sydney.
Remember?
Debbie: Oh, right. What time is it there?
John: It's 10:00 P.M. And it's four o'clock
there in Los Angeles. Right?
Debbie: Yes – four o'clock in the morning.
John: 4:00 A.M.? Oh, I'm really sorry.
Debbie: That's OK. I'm awake . . . now.

2 TELLING TIME (1)

A Listen and practice.

It's five o'clock **in the morning**.
It's 5:00 A.M.

It's seven o'clock **in the morning**.
It's 7:00 A.M.

It's twelve o'clock.
It's **noon**.

It's four **in the afternoon**.
It's 4:00 P.M.

It's seven **in the evening**.
It's 7:00 P.M.

It's twelve o'clock **at night**.
It's **midnight**.

B *Pair work* Say each time another way.

1. It's eight o'clock in the evening. *"It's 8:00 P.M."*
2. It's twelve o'clock at night.
3. It's three in the afternoon.
4. It's 3:00 A.M.
5. It's 6:00 P.M.
6. It's 4:00 P.M.

3 SNAPSHOT

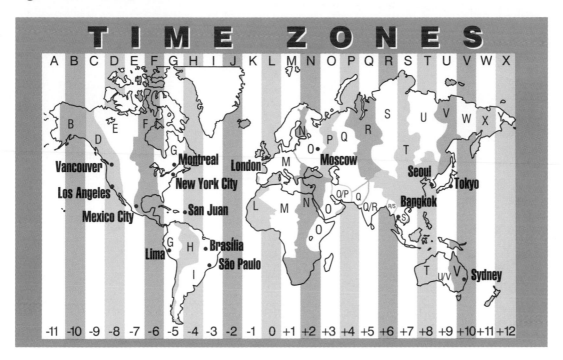

Listen and practice.

What time is it right now in your hometown?
What time is it in the cities on the map?

4 LISTENING

Tracy and Eric are calling friends in different parts of the world. Listen. What time is it in these cities?

CLASS AUDIO ONLY

City	Time
Vancouver	4:00 P.M.
Bangkok	
Tokyo	
São Paulo	

5 TELLING TIME (2)

A 💿 Listen and practice.

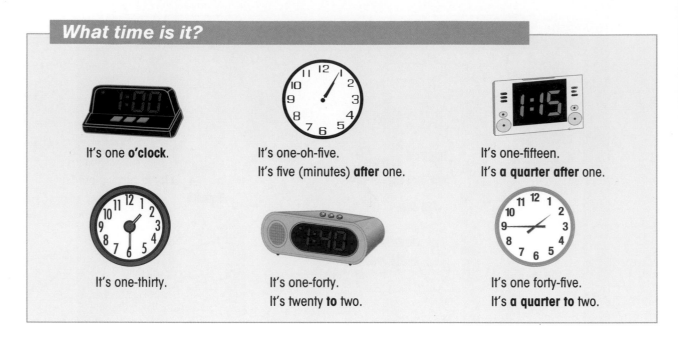

What time is it?

It's one **o'clock**.

It's one-oh-five.
It's five (minutes) **after** one.

It's one-fifteen.
It's **a quarter after** one.

It's one-thirty.

It's one-forty.
It's twenty **to** two.

It's one forty-five.
It's **a quarter to** two.

B *Pair work* Look at these clocks. What time is it?

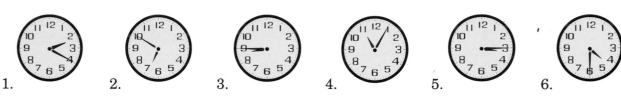

1.   2.   3.   4.   5.   6.

A: What time is it?
B: It's twenty after two. **OR** It's two-twenty.

6 CONVERSATION

💿 Listen and practice.

Steve: Hi, Mom.
Mrs. Dole: What are you doing, Steve?
Steve: I'm hungry, so I'm cooking.
Mrs. Dole: You're cooking? It's two o'clock in the morning!
Steve: Yeah, but I'm *really* hungry!
Mrs. Dole: What are you making?
Steve: Pizza.
Mrs. Dole: Mmm, pizza. So let's eat!

7 GRAMMAR FOCUS What + doing; *conjunction* so

Los Angeles 4:00 A.M.

What's Victoria **doing**?
She**'s sleeping** right now.

Mexico City 6:00 A.M.

What's Marcos **doing**?
It's 6:00 A.M., **so** he**'s getting up**.

New York City 7:00 A.M.

What are Sue and Tom **doing**?
They**'re having** breakfast.

Brasília 9:00 A.M.

What's Celia **doing**?
She**'s going** to work.

London 12:00 NOON

What are James and Anne **doing**?
It's noon, **so** they**'re having** lunch.

Moscow 3:00 P.M.

What's Andrei **doing**?
He**'s working**.

Bangkok 7:00 P.M.

What's Permsak **doing**?
He**'s eating** dinner right now.

Tokyo 9:00 P.M.

What's Hiroshi **doing**?
He's **watching** television.

Your city 00:00

What are you **doing**?
It's . . . , **so I'm** . . . .

A *Pair work* Ask and answer the questions about the pictures.

1. What time is it in Los Angeles?
2. What's Victoria doing?
3. Where are Sue and Tom?
4. Who's wearing pajamas? suits?
5. Who's working right now?
6. What's Marcos doing?
7. What's Celia doing?
8. Who's eating right now?

Spelling
sleep → sleep**ing**
get → get**ting** (+ *t*)
have → hav**ing** (– *e*)

B *Group work* Write five more questions about the pictures.
Ask and answer your questions in groups.

8 PRONUNCIATION Intonation of yes/no and Wh-questions

A 🔊 Listen and practice. Notice the intonation of the questions.

A: Is Victoria getting up?
B: No, she isn't.

A: What's Victoria doing?
B: She's sleeping.

B 🔊 Listen to the questions. Write ⤴ for rising intonation or ⤵ for falling intonation.

1. ⤴   2. ....   3. ....   4. ....   5. ....   6. ....

9 WORD POWER Activities

A 🔊 Listen and practice. *"He's playing tennis."*

 play tennis
 ride a bike
 run
 swim
 take a walk
 dance

 drive
 go to the movies
 shop
 read
 study
 watch television

B *Group work* Take turns acting out the verbs and guessing the actions.

A: *(acting out dancing)*
B: Are you swimming?
A: No, I'm not.

C: Are you dancing?
A: Yes, I am.

10 LISTENING

A 🔊 What's Debbie doing? Listen to the sounds and number the actions from 1 to 8.

..... dancing   ..... eating dinner   ..... riding a bike   ..... swimming
1 driving   ..... playing tennis   ..... shopping   ..... watching television

B 🔊 Listen again and ask and answer questions about each sound.

A: What's Debbie doing right now?
B: She's driving.

11 *READING*

It's Saturday! What are you doing?

Read the first sentence of each paragraph. Find the picture for each paragraph.

a

b

c

d

1. ...*d*... We're washing people's cars. My friends and I are working together. The money from the car wash is for our school football team.

2. .... I'm watching a funny movie with my friend. It's noon. My friend is laughing at something, so now I'm laughing, too. We're laughing at *everything*!

3. .... I'm with my granddaughter in the park. Her parents are working today. We're playing and talking. She's telling me about school. She and I are good friends.

4. .... I'm sitting in bed with my laptop computer. It's 11:00 at night. I'm writing letters to friends. They're in other countries. But I'm thinking about them, so I'm not sad.

A Read the article. Then add these clauses to the appropriate paragraph.

1. . . . , so she's with me for the day.
   Her parents are working today,
   so she's with me for the day.
2. . . . , so I'm not working.
3. . . . , so the movie theater isn't full.
4. . . . , so the work is actually fun.

B *Group work* Imagine it is Saturday. You and your classmates are together. Where are you? What are you doing? Write five sentences.

We're in the park. We're riding our bikes. . . .

interchange 5

Time zones

What are people doing in different cities of the world? Turn to page IC-8.

6 We live in the suburbs.

1 SNAPSHOT

🔊 Listen and practice.

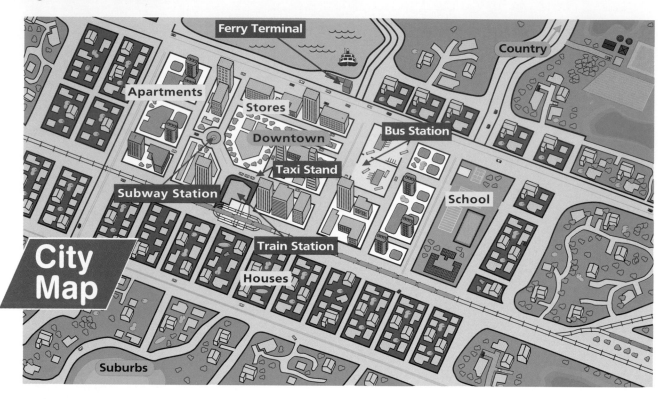

City Map

Ferry Terminal

Country

Apartments

Stores

Downtown

Bus Station

Taxi Stand

Subway Station

School

Train Station

Houses

Suburbs

Which of these places are in your hometown?
What public transportation do you have? buses?
  trains? a subway? taxis? ferries?
Can you name other places in your hometown?

2 CONVERSATION

🔊 Listen and practice.

Ashley: Hey, Jason. What are you doing?
Jason: Oh, I'm waiting for my mom.
   My bike has a flat tire.
Ashley: Is she coming right now?
Jason: Yeah. She works near here.
Ashley: Oh, that's good.
Jason: So what are *you* doing?
Ashley: I'm going home. I don't live far
   from here, so I walk to school.
Jason: You're lucky!

34

3 WORD POWER *Family relationships*

A 📟 *Pair work* Complete the sentences about
the Carter family. Then listen to check your answers.

1. Anne is Charles's .....*wife*..... .
2. Jason and Emily are their ....
3. Charles is Anne's............ .
4. Jason is Anne's............ .
5. Emily is Charles's ....
6. Jason is Emily's ....
7. Emily is Jason's ....
8. Charles and Anne are
   Jason's ....

kids	=	children
mom	=	mother
dad	=	father

B *Pair work* Tell your partner
about your family.

"My mother's name is Angela.
David and Daniel are my brothers."

The Carter Family

husband wife

parents / children

father / son

mother / daughter

brother sister

Charles   Jason   Emily   Anne

4 GRAMMAR FOCUS

Simple present statements 📟						
I	**walk**	to school.	I	**don't live**	far from here.	**don't = do not**
You	**ride**	your bike to school.	You	**don't live**	near here.	**doesn't = does not**
He	**works**	near here.	He	**doesn't work**	downtown.	
She	**takes**	the bus to work.	She	**doesn't drive**	to work.	
We	**live**	with our parents.	We	**don't live**	alone.	
They	**use**	public transportation.	They	**don't need**	a car.	

A Charles Carter is talking about his family. Complete the sentences.
Choose the correct verb form. Then compare with a partner.

1. My family and I ...*live*.... (live / lives) in the suburbs. My wife ....
   (work / works) near here, so she .... (drive / drives) to her office. I
   .... (don't / doesn't) work in the suburbs. I .... (take / takes) the
   bus to the city. Our son .... (ride / rides) his bike to school, but
   our daughter .... (don't / doesn't) go to school yet.

2. My parents .... (live / lives) in the city. My mother ....
   (take / takes) a train to work. My father .... (don't / doesn't) work
   now. He's retired. He also .... (use / uses) public transportation,
   so they .... (don't / doesn't) need a car.

Simple present statements with irregular verbs

I/you/we/they	he/she/it
I **have** a bike.	It **has** a flat tire.
We **do** our homework every day.	My father **does** a lot of work at home.
My parents **go** to work by car.	My sister **goes** to school by bus.

B Ashley is talking about her family and her friend Jason. Complete the sentences. Then compare with a partner.

1. I live with my parents. We ..*have*.. (have/has) a house in the suburbs. My mom and dad both .... (go/goes) downtown to work. They both .... (have/has) cars and drive to work every day. I .... (do/does) a lot of work at home because my parents are very busy.

2. My brother doesn't live with us. He .... (have/has) an apartment in the city. He .... (go/goes) to school all day, and he .... (do/does) office work at night.

3. I .... (have/has) a new friend. His name is Jason. He doesn't have a car, but he .... (have/has) a cool bike. Jason and I .... (do/does) our homework together after school.

---

 5 *LISTENING*

Pair work How do these people go to work or school? Do they walk? take the bus? ride a bike? drive? Write one guess in the chart for each person.  Then listen and complete the chart.

CLASS
AUDIO
ONLY ▶

Jeremy

Tina

Rosie

Louis

Your guess	How they actually go to work or school
Jeremy *rides a bike to school.*	Jeremy ....
Tina	Tina ....
Rosie	Rosie ....
Louis	Louis ....

6 PRONUNCIATION *Third-person singular* s

 Listen and practice. Notice the pronunciation of **s** endings.

s = /s/		s = /z/		(e)s = /ɪz/		*irregular*	
take	take**s**	go	goe**s**	dance	dance**s**	do	doe**s**
sit	sit**s**	live	live**s**	use	use**s**	say	say**s**
walk	walk**s**	study	stud**ies**	watch	watch**es**	have	ha**s**

7 WHO IS IT?

A Write five sentences about you, your family, and your friends. Write "Male" or "Female" on your paper, but not your name.

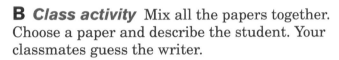

(Female) I live with my parents. I have two sisters. We go to Europe in the summer. . . .

B *Class activity* Mix all the papers together. Choose a paper and describe the student. Your classmates guess the writer.

A: "She lives with her parents. She has two sisters. They go to Europe in the summer. . . ." Who is it?
B: Is it Michelle?
C: No, it's not me.
D: Is it Christine?
E: Yes, it's me!

8 CONVERSATION

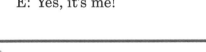 Listen and practice.

Jack: Let's go to the park on Sunday.
Amy: OK, but let's not go early. I sleep late on weekends.
Jack: What time do you get up on Sundays?
Amy: At ten o'clock.
Jack: Oh, that isn't very late. I get up at noon.
Amy: Do you eat breakfast then?
Jack: Sure. I have breakfast every day.
Amy: Then let's meet at Harry's Restaurant at one o'clock. They serve breakfast all day on Sundays – for people like us.

9 LISTENING *Days of the week*

CLASS
AUDIO
ONLY ▶ **A** 📼 Listen and practice.

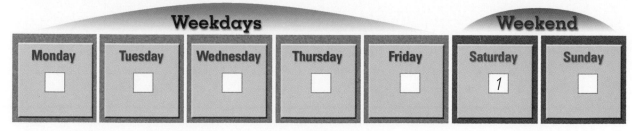

Weekdays | Weekend

Monday	Tuesday	Wednesday	Thursday	Friday	Saturday	Sunday
☐	☐	☐	☐	☐	*1*	☐

CLASS
AUDIO
ONLY ▶ **B** 📼 Listen to four conversations. What days do the people talk about? Write the number of the conversation on the day of the week.

10 GRAMMAR FOCUS

Simple present questions 📼

Do you **get up** early on weekends?	No, I **get up** late.
What time **do** you **get up**?	At ten o'clock.
Does he **have** breakfast on Sundays?	Yes, he **eats** breakfast every day.
What time **does** he **have** breakfast?	At noon.
Do they **shop** together?	Yes, they **shop** together a lot.
When **do** they **shop**?	On Saturdays.

Time expressions

early	**on** Sundays	**in** the morning	**at** nine o'clock
late	**on** weekends	**in** the afternoon	**at** noon/**at** midnight
every day	**on** weekdays	**in** the evening	**at** night

A *Pair work* Ask and answer questions about your daily life. Add three more questions to the list.

1. What time do you get up? Do you get up early on weekends?
2. How do you go to school or work? Do you take the bus?
3. What time do you go home? Do you eat with your family?
4. When do you have English class?
5. Do you see your friends in the evening? Do you call your friends?
6. Do you have a computer at home? Do you go on the Internet at night?
7. What time do you go to bed?
8. ....
9. ....
10. ....

B *Class activity* Are you and your partner the same or different? Tell the class.

"Wen Pin and I get up early on weekdays. Wen Pin gets up early on weekends, but I get up late. . . ."

11 *READING*

WHAT'S YOUR SCHEDULE LIKE?

Look at the pictures. Who gets up early? Who gets up late?

Brittany Davis
College Student

"My classes all start at 8:00 A.M., so I get up at 7:00, eat a quick breakfast, and take the bus to the university. In the afternoon, I have a job at the library. My only time to study is in the evening, from eight until midnight. I work at the library on Saturdays, too. But on Saturday nights I stay out late, and on Sundays I sleep until noon!"

Joshua Burns
Web-Site Designer

"I design Web sites for small companies. I'm self-employed, so I work at home. I get up at 6:30 and go for a run before breakfast. I'm at my computer by 8:00, and I work until 6:00. Around one o'clock, I take a lunch break, and I 'surf the Net' to look at other Web sites. I work hard – sometimes I work all night to finish a project. But I never work on weekends!"

Maya Black
Rock Musician

"I go to work at ten o'clock in the evening, and I play until 3:00 A.M. I take a break at midnight, though. After work, I have dinner at an all-night restaurant. Then I take a taxi home. I go to bed at five in the morning and sleep until two in the afternoon. I only work three nights a week – Friday, Saturday, and Sunday – but I practice every afternoon."

A Read the article and answer the questions.

1. What time does each person get up?
2. Who works on weekends? Who works on weekdays?
3. Who eats breakfast in the morning?
4. Who works five days a week?
5. Find one thing you like about each person's schedule.
6. Find one thing you don't like about each person's schedule.

B *Pair work* Write five sentences about your schedule. Compare with a partner. Are you an "early bird" or a "night owl"? (Early birds get up early in the morning. Night owls stay up late at night.)

interchange 6

Class survey
Find out more about your classmates. Turn to page IC-9.

7 Does the apartment have a view?

1 SNAPSHOT

 Listen and practice.

Houses and Apartments

second floor

bedroom   bedroom

closet   hall   stairs

bedroom   bathroom

first floor

dining room   laundry room

kitchen

living room

stairs   garage

yard

House

bathroom

bedroom   closet

dining room   kitchen

living room   elevator

Apartment

lobby

Which rooms are in houses in your country?
Which rooms are in apartments in your country?

2 CONVERSATION

 Listen and practice.

Linda: Guess what! I have a new apartment.
Chris: That's super. What's it like?
Linda: It's really beautiful.
Chris: How many rooms does it have?
Linda: Well, it has a bedroom, a bathroom, a kitchen, and a living room. Oh, and a big closet in the hall.
Chris: Where is it?
Linda: It's on Lakeview Drive.
Chris: Oh, nice. Does it have a view?
Linda: Yes, it does. It has a great view of my neighbor's apartment!

40

3 GRAMMAR FOCUS

Simple present short answers; how many

Do you **live** in an apartment?
Yes, I **do**.
No, I **don't**.

Does the apartment **have** a view?
Yes, it **does**.
No, it **doesn't**.

Do the bedrooms **have** closets?
Yes, they **do**.
No, they **don't**.

How many rooms **does** the apartment **have**?
It **has** four rooms.

A Complete the conversation. Then practice with a partner.

Linda: ...*Do*... you ...*live*... in an apartment?
Chris: No, I .... I .... in a house.
Linda: What's it like? .... it .... a yard?
Chris: Yes, it .... And it's next to the river.
Linda: That sounds nice. .... you .... alone?
Chris: No, I .... I .... with my parents and my sisters.
Linda: How many sisters .... you .... ?
Chris: I .... four.
Linda: That's a big family. .... you .... a big house?
Chris: Yes, we .... It .... ten rooms.
Linda: Ten rooms! How many bedrooms .... it .... ?
Chris: It .... four.
Linda: .... you .... your own bedroom?
Chris: Yes, I .... I'm really lucky.

B *Pair work* Read the conversation in part A again. Ask and answer these questions. For "no" answers, give the correct information.

1. Does Chris live in an apartment?
   "No, he doesn't. He lives in a house."
2. Does Chris's home have a yard?
3. Does Chris live alone?
4. Does he have four brothers?
5. Does he have his own room?

C Write five questions like the ones in part B about a partner's home. Ask and answer your questions with your partner.

4 LISTENING

 Listen to people describe their homes. Number the pictures from 1 to 4.

5 WORD POWER Furniture

A 📼 Listen and practice.

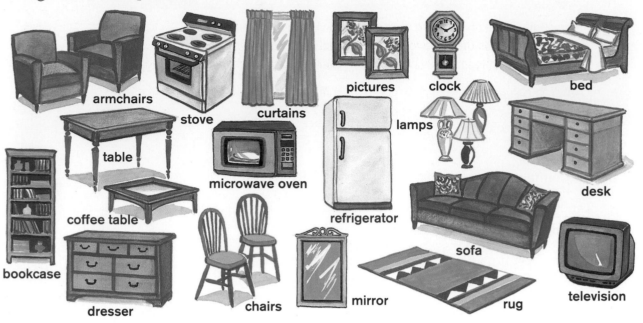

armchairs
stove
curtains
pictures
clock
bed
table
microwave oven
lamps
refrigerator
desk
coffee table
sofa
bookcase
dresser
chairs
mirror
rug
television

B Where do these things go? Complete the chart.

Kitchen	*table* *stove*
Dining room	*table*
Living room	
Bedroom	

C *Group work* Compare your charts.

A: The table goes in the kitchen.
B: The table goes in the dining room, too.

6 CONVERSATION

📼 Listen and practice.

Chris: This apartment is great.
Linda: Thanks. I love it, but I really need some furniture.
Chris: What do you need?
Linda: Well, there are some chairs in the kitchen, but there isn't a table.
Chris: And there's no sofa here in the living room.
Linda: And there aren't any chairs. There's only this lamp.
Chris: So let's go shopping next weekend!

7 GRAMMAR FOCUS

There is, there are 🔊

There's a lamp in the living room.
There's no sofa in the living room.
There isn't a table in the kitchen.

There are some chairs in the kitchen.
There are no chairs in the living room.
There aren't any chairs in the living room.

There's = There is

A Say each sentence another way.

1. I don't have a table in the kitchen. *"There's no table in the kitchen."*
2. I have some chairs in the kitchen. *"There are some chairs in the kitchen."*
3. I have a stove in the kitchen.
4. I don't have a refrigerator.
5. I have some curtains on the windows.
6. I don't have any rugs on the floor.

B *Pair work* Look at the picture of Linda's apartment. Take turns saying what things Linda has and doesn't have in her apartment.

A: There's a mirror in the bedroom.
B: But there aren't any pictures in the bedroom.

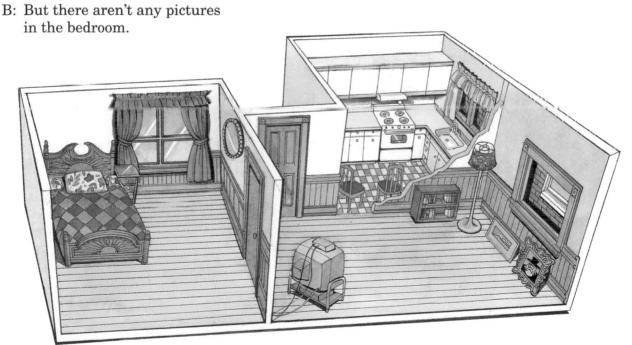

C Write five sentences about things you have or don't have in your classroom and school. Then compare with a partner.

There are twenty desks in the classroom.
There aren't any computers.

8 PRONUNCIATION *Words with* th

A Listen and practice. Notice the two pronunciations of **th**.

/ð/   /θ/   /ð/   /ð/   /θ/   /θ/
There are **th**irteen rooms in **th**is house. **Th**e house has **th**ree ba**th**rooms.

B Think of three other /ð/ words and three other /θ/ words.
Write three funny sentences using them, and read them aloud.

> *On Thursdays, their mother and father think for thirteen minutes.*

9 LISTENING

CLASS AUDIO ONLY ▶ Listen to Linda and Chris shopping. What does Linda buy?
Check (✓) the things.

What does Linda buy?			
✓ chairs	☐ a sofa	☐ a rug	☐ a table
☐ a refrigerator	☐ a dresser	☐ a coffee table	☐ curtains

10 DREAM HOUSE

A Write a description of your dream house.

Where is your dream house?
How many rooms does it have?
What are the rooms?
What's in the rooms?
What else does it have?

> *My dream house is in the country.*
> *There are twenty rooms. . . .*

B *Pair work* Ask your partner about
his or her dream house.

A: Does it have a swimming pool?
B: Yes, it does. There's a really big pool.

patio

swimming pool

trees

balcony

porch

garage

yard

garden

11 READING

TWO SPECIAL HOUSES IN THE AMERICAN SOUTHWEST

Look at the pictures. What is special about the two houses?

In San Antonio, Texas, there is a purple house. This house is the home of Sandra Cisneros. Ms. Cisneros is a Mexican-American writer. She is famous for her interesting stories. The house has a porch with a pink floor. The rooms are green, pink, and purple. There are many books and colorful paintings. Many other houses near Ms. Cisneros's house are white or beige, so her house is very different. Some of her neighbors think her house is too colorful, but Ms. Cisneros loves it.

Every year many people visit the land of the Navajos, the largest Native American tribe in the Southwest. Most people stay in hotels, but some are now staying in traditional Navajo homes, called *hogans*. Hogans are made of logs and mud and have dirt floors. Lorraine Nelson, a schoolteacher from Arizona, now invites visitors to stay in a hogan on her property. Her hogan has three chairs, two beds on the floor, and a wood-burning stove. Ms. Nelson teaches guests about Navajo traditions.

A Read the article. What's in the two houses? Complete the chart.

three chairs   colorful paintings   two beds on the floor
many books   ✓porch with a pink floor   wood-burning stove

Sandra Cisneros's house	Lorraine Nelson's hogan
1. There is a *porch with a pink floor* .	4. There is a ....
2. There are	5. There are ....
3. There are	6. There are ....

B *Group work* Talk about these questions.

1. Imagine that you want to paint your house. What colors do you choose? Why?
2. Imagine that you are visiting Arizona. Do you stay in a hogan or in a hotel? Why?

Find the differences
Compare two apartments.
Turn to page
IC-10.

What do you do?

1 WORD POWER Jobs

A 🔊 Listen and practice. Then match the occupations to the pictures. *"He's a receptionist."*

a. cashier	e. judge	i. pilot	m. security guard
b. cook/chef	f . lawyer	j. police officer	n. singer
c. doctor	g. musician	✓k. receptionist	o. waiter
d. flight attendant	h. nurse	l. salesperson	p. waitress

1. k 2. ☐ 3. ☐

4. ☐ 5. ☐

6. ☐ 7. ☐

8. ☐ 9. ☐ 10. ☐

11. ☐ 12. ☐ 13. ☐

14. ☐ 15. ☐ 16. ☐

B *Pair work* Compare your answers.

A: What's his job?
B: He's a receptionist.

2 THE WORLD OF WORK

A *Pair work* Who works in these places? Complete the chart with occupations from Exercise 1. Add one more occupation to each list.

A: A doctor works in a hospital.
B: A nurse works in a hospital, too.

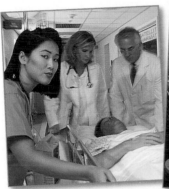

In a hospital	In an office	In a store	In a hotel
doctor			
nurse			

B *Class activity* Ask and answer questions about occupations.

Who ... ?
- wears a uniform
- stands all day
- sits all day
- handles money
- talks to people
- works hard
- works at night
- carries a gun

A: Who wears a uniform?
B: A police officer wears a uniform.
C: And a security guard . . . .

3 CONVERSATION

 Listen and practice.

Rachel: Where does your brother work?
Angela: In a hotel.
Rachel: Oh, that's interesting. My brother works in a hotel, too.
Angela: Really? What does he do, exactly?
Rachel: He's a chef in the restaurant. What about your brother?
Angela: He's a security guard, but he doesn't like it.
Rachel: That's too bad.
Angela: Yeah. He's looking for a new job.

4 GRAMMAR FOCUS

Simple present Wh-questions with do 🔊

Where do you work?	Where does she work?	Where do they work?
I work in a hotel.	She works in a store.	They work in a hospital.
What do you do there?	**What does she do** there?	**What do they do** there?
I'm a receptionist.	She's a cashier.	They're nurses.

a doctor · a salesperson · a computer repairperson

Complete these conversations with questions.
Then practice with a partner.

1. A: *What does your sister do* ?
   B: My sister? She's a doctor.
   A: .... ?
   B: In a hospital. And she has an office, too.

2. A: .... ?
   B: I work in an electronics store.
   A: .... , exactly?
   B: I sell CD players, televisions, and telephones.

3. A: .... ?
   B: Tom works in a computer factory.
   A: .... there, exactly?
   B: He's a repairperson. He repairs computers.

5 PRONUNCIATION Reduction of do and does

A 🔊 Listen and practice. Notice the reduction of **do** and **does** in these questions.

Where **do you** work?   What **do you** do?
Where **does he** work?   What **does he** do?
Where **do they** work?   What **do they** do?

B Practice the conversations in Exercise 4 again. Pay attention to your pronunciation of **do you**, **does she**, and **does he**.

6 WORKDAYS

Group work Ask three classmates about their jobs.
If they don't have a job, ask them about a friend or family
member. Then tell the class.

Ask about a classmate
Do you have a job?
Where do you work?
What do you do, exactly?
What time do you start work?
When do you finish work?
Do you take a break in the afternoon?
What do you do after work?
Do you watch television? read?
 study?

"Victor is a cashier. He works in a
department store. He starts work
at 10:00 A.M., and he finishes at
6:00 P.M. . . ."

**Ask about a classmate's
friend or relative**
Tell me about your brother
 (sister). . . .
Where does he work?
What does he do, exactly?
What time does he start work?
When does he finish work?
Does he like his job?
What does he do after work? . . .

"Tomoko doesn't have a job,
but her brother is a waiter. He
works in a restaurant. He starts
work . . . ."

7 SNAPSHOT

Job Survey	Exciting	Boring	Easy	Difficult	Safe	Dangerous	Relaxing	Stressful
actor				X				
air traffic controller								X
artist							X	
athlete	X							
carpenter						X		
DJ (disc jockey)			X					
fashion designer	X							
flight attendant		X						
florist					X			
gardener							X	
librarian					X			
pilot						X		
police officer						X		
receptionist		X						
teacher				X				
waiter/waitress								X

People's opinions of different jobs

Source: Interviews with people between the ages of 18 and 50

Complete the chart with your opinions.
Which opinions do you agree with?
Which opinions do you disagree with? Why?

8 CONVERSATION

 Listen and practice.

Richard: Hi, Stephanie. I hear you have a new job.
Stephanie: Yes. I'm teaching math at Lincoln High School.
Richard: How do you like it?
Stephanie: It's great. The students are terrific. How are things with you?
Richard: Not bad. I'm an air traffic controller now, you know.
Stephanie: Now, that's exciting!
Richard: Yes, but it's a very stressful job.

9 GRAMMAR FOCUS

Adjectives before nouns

be + adjective	adjective + noun
A police officer's job **is dangerous**.	A police officer has **a dangerous job**.
A doctor's job **is stressful**.	A doctor has **a stressful job**.

A *Pair work* Say each sentence another way.

1. A photographer's job is interesting.
   "A photographer has an interesting job."
2. An athlete's job is exciting.
3. A lawyer's job is stressful.
4. A gardener's job is relaxing.
5. An accountant's job is difficult.
6. A firefighter's job is dangerous.

B *Class activity* Think of two jobs for each category. Do you and your classmates agree?

a boring job	....	....
an easy job	....	....
a dangerous job	....	....
an exciting job	....	....
a difficult job	....	....
a stressful job	....	....

A: A musician has a boring job.
B: I disagree. A rock musician doesn't have a boring job.
C: I agree. A rock musician's job is very exciting.

a photographer

an accountant

a firefighter

10 LISTENING

Listen to these women talk about their jobs. Number the pictures from 1 to 4. Then listen again. Are their jobs boring, stressful, difficult, easy, or exciting? Write the correct adjective under the picture.

....

....

<u>1</u>

...........*boring*...........

....

11 READING

What do you do, exactly?

Cover the reading and look at the pictures. What does each person do?

Joseph Todd

As a judge, I am in charge of trials. I listen to people and their lawyers, and I make decisions. These decisions are sometimes very difficult. Of course, I know the law well, but each person's case is different, and I try to be fair.

Molly Swift

I do many kinds of carpentry. That way, I work all year. I build furniture, and I also build houses. My work is sometimes difficult and dangerous. These days, a lot of things are "prefabricated" – already made. As a result, my job is easier, but there is less work.

Benjamin Morse

My job keeps me busy. I plan lessons, give tests, grade homework, talk to parents, help with after-school activities – and, of course, I teach! My salary isn't great, but that's OK. My students are excited about learning, so I'm happy.

A Read the article. Who do you think says this? Write the name of the person.

1. "Sometimes I work a lot, but sometimes I don't." ....
2. "This year, I'm helping with the soccer team." ....
3. "I'm not always happy about my decisions." ....

B *Group work* Write a description of a job in two or three sentences. Can the other people in your group guess the job?

"Every year, many people see me. I'm always playing other people." (actor)

interchange 8

The perfect job

What do you want in a job? Turn to page IC-11.

Review of Units 5–8

CLASS
AUDIO
ONLY

1 LISTENING

Pair work Victoria is calling friends in different parts of the world. Where are they? What time is it there? What are they doing? Complete the chart.

Victoria   Sue   Marcos   Jim

	City	Time	Activity
1. Sue	....	....	....
2. Marcos	....	....	....
3. Jim	....	....	....

2 TRUE OR FALSE?

A Write three true statements and one false statement about your classroom.

> *Our classroom has a nice view.*
> *There's a cassette player on the teacher's desk.*

It has . . . .
It doesn't have . . . .
There's a/an . . . .
There are . . . .
There isn't a/an . . . .
There's no . . . .
There aren't any . . . .
There are no . . . .

B *Pair work* Take turns reading your statements. Say "True" or "False" for each statement. For false statements, give the true information.

A: Our classroom has a nice view.
B: False. There aren't any windows in our classroom.

3 HABITS

A Write eight sentences about yourself. Name two things . . . .

you do in the morning   you do on weekends
you don't do in the morning   you don't do on weekends

> *I have breakfast in the morning.*

B *Group work* Compare. Who has similar habits?

A: What do you do in the morning?   C: What don't you do in the morning?
B: I have breakfast in the morning.   B: I don't read the newspaper.

4 WHAT'S THE QUESTION?

A Look at these answers. What are the questions?
Write them down. Then compare with a partner.

1. A: *Where do you work?*
   B: I work in a store.
2. A: ....
   B: I'm a salesperson.
3. A: ....
   B: I really like my job.
4. A: ....
   B: I live in an apartment downtown.
5. A: ....
   B: My apartment has five rooms.

6. A: ....
   B: I need a sofa, a rug, and a lamp.
7. A: ....
   B: I go to class by subway.
8. A: ....
   B: I get up at 6:00 A.M. every morning.
9. A: ....
   B: It's four o'clock in the morning!
10. A: ....
    B: I'm watching television right now.

B *Pair work* Take turns. Ask the questions in part A.
Answer with your own information.

5 TWENTY QUESTIONS

Group work Take turns. One student thinks of a
famous person. The group asks up to twenty questions like
the ones below. The student answers with "Yes" or "No."

Is it a man?/Is it a woman?
Does he/she live in the United States?
Is he/she Canadian?
Is he/she a singer/an actor/. . . ?
Does he/she wear glasses?
Is he/she young/middle-aged/old?

When you think you know the person's
name, ask, "Is his/her name . . . ?"

9 Broccoli is good for you.

SNAPSHOT

Listen and practice.

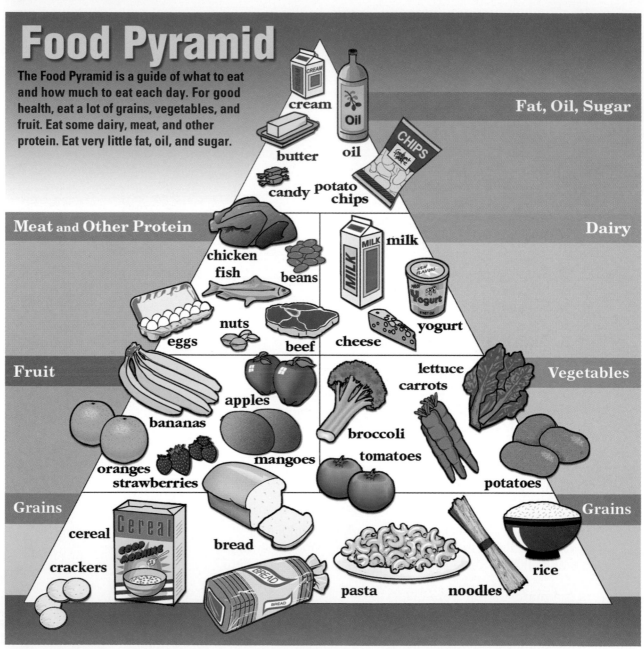

Food Pyramid

The Food Pyramid is a guide of what to eat and how much to eat each day. For good health, eat a lot of grains, vegetables, and fruit. Eat some dairy, meat, and other protein. Eat very little fat, oil, and sugar.

Fat, Oil, Sugar

cream
Oil
butter
oil
candy   potato chips
CHIPS

Meat and Other Protein

Dairy

chicken
fish
beans
milk
MILK   MILK
Yogurt
nuts
yogurt
eggs
beef
cheese

Fruit

Vegetables

apples
bananas
broccoli
lettuce
carrots
oranges
strawberries
mangoes
tomatoes
potatoes

Grains

Grains

cereal
Cereal
bread
crackers
BREAD
pasta
noodles
rice

Source: Adapted from the U.S. Department of Agriculture Food Guide Pyramid

According to this Food Pyramid, which foods are good for you? bad for you?
Do you agree with the idea of a Food Pyramid?
Which foods do you eat? Which foods don't you eat?

2 WORD POWER *Foods: countable and uncountable*

A 🔊 Listen and practice.

	specific	general
Countable ⟶	I'm buying **an orange**.*	I love **oranges**. **Oranges** are delicious.
Uncountable ⟶	I'm buying **some broccoli**.	I like **broccoli**. **Broccoli** is good for you.

*Note: Singular = "I'm buying **an orange**." Plural = "I'm buying **some oranges**."

B Divide the words in the Food Pyramid into two lists: countable and uncountable nouns. Add two more foods to each list.

Countable (singular and plural)		Uncountable (only singular)	
bananas		*beef*	

C *Pair work* Complete these general statements with **is** or **are**. Then rewrite the sentences with your own information. Compare with a partner.

1. Carrots ....*are*.... my favorite vegetable.
2. I think mangoes .... delicious.
3. Broccoli .... very good for you.
4. Strawberries .... my favorite fruit.
5. I think yogurt .... awful.
6. Chicken .... my favorite meat.

A: Tomatoes are my favorite vegetable.
B: Broccoli is my favorite vegetable.

3 CONVERSATION

A Listen and practice.

Adam: What do you want for the barbecue?
Amanda: Hmm. How about chicken and hamburgers?
Adam: OK. We have some chicken in the freezer, but we don't have any hamburger meat.
Amanda: And there aren't any hamburger rolls.
Adam: Do we have any soda?
Amanda: No, we don't. We need some. Oh, and let's get some lemonade, too.
Adam: All right. And how about potato salad?
Amanda: Oh, yeah. Everyone likes potato salad.

CLASS AUDIO ONLY

B Listen to the rest of the conversation. Check (✓) the desserts Adam and Amanda want for their barbecue.

☐ fruit salad   ☐ pie   ☐ ice cream
☐ cake   ☐ cookies

4 GRAMMAR FOCUS

CLASS AUDIO ONLY

Some *and* any

Do we need **any** meat?	We need **some** hamburger meat.	We don't need **any** chicken.
Do we need **any** soda?	Yes, let's get **some** soda.	No, we don't need **any** soda.
	Yes, let's get **some**.	No, we don't need **any**.

Note: *Some* and *any* are also used with plural countable nouns:
"Do you want **some** bananas?" "No, I don't want **any**."

Complete this conversation with **some** or **any**.
Then compare with a partner.

Amanda: Hmm. Let's not buy ...*any*... potato salad.
Let's make ..*some*.. at home.
Adam: OK. So we need .... potatoes.
Is there .... mayonnaise at home?
Amanda: No, we need to buy ....
Adam: OK. And we need .... onions, too.
Amanda: Oh, I don't want .... onions in the salad. I hate onions!
Adam: Then let's buy .... celery. That's delicious in potato salad.
Amanda: Good idea. And .... carrots, too.

5 *PRONUNCIATION* Sentence stress

A Listen and practice. Notice the words with the most stress.

A: What do you **néed**?
B: I need some **bréad** and some **físh**.
A: Do you need any **frúit**?
B: **Yés**. I want some ba**ná**nas.

B What do you need from the grocery store today? Make a list. Then compare your list with a partner.

6 *CONVERSATION*

Listen and practice.

Sarah: Let's have breakfast together on Sunday.
Kumiko: OK. Come to my house. My family always has a Japanese-style breakfast on Sundays.
Sarah: Really? What do you have?
Kumiko: We usually have fish, rice, and soup.
Sarah: Fish for breakfast? That's interesting.
Kumiko: Sometimes we have a salad, too. And we always have green tea.
Sarah: Well, I never eat fish for breakfast, but I love to try new things.

7 *GRAMMAR FOCUS*

Adverbs of frequency

I **always** eat breakfast. usually often sometimes seldom never **Sometimes** I eat breakfast.	Do you **ever** have fish for breakfast? Yes, I **always** do. **Sometimes** I do. No, I **never** do.	**100%** always usually often sometimes seldom **0%** never

A Add the adverbs in the correct places. Then practice with a partner.

        usually
A: What do you have for breakfast? (usually)
B: Well, on Sundays I have eggs, bacon, and toast. (often)
A: Do you eat breakfast at work? (ever)
B: I have breakfast at my desk. (sometimes)
A: Do you eat rice for breakfast? (usually)
B: No, I have rice. (seldom)

57

B *Pair work* Put the words in order to make sentences. Then rewrite the sentences with your own information. Compare with a partner.

1. ...*I never have breakfast on weekends.*...................
   I   never   breakfast   on   have   weekends
2. ....
   work   I   snacks   eat   at   seldom
3. ....
   eat   for   pasta   dinner   sometimes   I
4. ....
   have   I   dinner   with   often   family   my

A: I always have breakfast on weekends.
B: I seldom have breakfast on weekends. I get up very late.

---

8 *LISTENING*

Listen to Paul and Megan talk about food. How often does Megan eat these foods? Check (✓) **often**, **sometimes**, or **never**.

	Often	Sometimes	Never
pasta	✓	☐	☐
hamburgers	☐	☐	☐
fish	☐	☐	☐
eggs	☐	☐	☐
broccoli	☐	☐	☐

---

9 *BREAKFAST, LUNCH, AND DINNER*

A *Pair work* Add three questions to the list. Then ask and answer the questions with a partner.

1. Do you usually have breakfast in the morning?
2. What time do you eat?
3. Do you ever eat meat or fish for breakfast?
4. Do you ever go to a restaurant for breakfast?
5. Do you always drink the same thing in the morning?
6. What is something you never have for breakfast?
7. ....
8. ....
9. ....

B *Group work* Ask and answer similar questions about lunch and dinner.

interchange 9

Eating habits
What foods do
you eat?
Turn to page IC-12.

10 READING

Eating for Good Luck

On special occasions, do you ever eat any of the foods in these pictures?

On New Year's Day, many people eat special foods for good luck in the new year.

Some Chinese people eat tangerines. Tangerines are round. Round foods end and begin again, like years.

It is a Jewish custom to eat apples with honey for a sweet new year.

Greeks eat *vasilopitta,* bread with a coin inside. Everyone tries to find the coin for luck and money in the new year.

In Spain and some Latin American countries, people eat twelve grapes at midnight on New Year's Eve – one grape for good luck in each month of the new year.

On New Year's Day in Japan, people eat *mochi* – rice cakes – for strength in the new year.

Some Americans from southern states eat black-eyed peas and rice with collard greens. The black-eyed peas are like coins, and the greens are like dollars.

A Read the article. Then correct the information in these sentences.

1. Some Chinese people eat tangerines. Tangerines are ~~sweet~~, like years. *round*
2. Some Jewish people eat apples with candy for a sweet new year.
3. Greeks eat vasilopitta, bread with beans inside.
4. In Europe, people eat twelve grapes for good luck in the new year.
5. The Japanese eat chocolate cake for strength in the new year.
6. Some Americans eat black-eyed peas. Black-eyed peas are like dollars.

B *Group work* Talk about these questions.

1. Do you eat anything special on New Year's Day for good luck? What?
2. Do you do anything special on New Year's Day for good luck? What?

10 You can play baseball really well.

SNAPSHOT

Listen and practice.

SPORTS SEASONS IN THE UNITED STATES AND CANADA

In the winter, people . . . .

play hockey
play basketball
go ice-skating
go skiing

In the spring, people . . . .

play golf
play soccer

In the summer, people . . . .

play baseball
play tennis
play volleyball
go swimming

In the fall, people . . . .

play football
go bike riding
go hiking

Sources: Adapted from *ESPN Information Please Sports Almanac*
and interviews with people between the ages of 18 and 50

What sports do people play in your country?
Do you like sports? What sports do you play?

2 CONVERSATION

 Listen and practice.

Lauren: So, Justin, what do you do in your free time?
Justin: Well, I love sports.
Lauren: Really? What sports do you like?
Justin: Hmm. Hockey, baseball, and skiing are my favorites.
Lauren: Wow, you're a really good athlete!
Justin: Oh, no, I'm not. I don't *play* those sports. I just watch them on TV!

3 GRAMMAR FOCUS

Simple present Wh-questions

What sports do you play?	I play **baseball** and I **go skiing**.
Who do you play baseball **with**?	**With some friends from work.** We have a team.
When does your team practice?	We practice **on Saturdays**.
What time do you practice on Saturdays?	We start **at ten o'clock in the morning**.
Where do you go skiing?	I go skiing **in Colorado**.
What do your parents **think of** skiing?	They **think it's dangerous**.

A Write questions for these answers. Then compare with a partner.

1. A: *What sports do you like?*
   B: I like ice-skating, but I really love volleyball!

2. A: ....
   B: Volleyball? I play it in the summer.

3. A: ....
   B: My brother and sister play with me.

4. A: ....
   B: We usually play in our yard or at the beach.

5. A: ....
   B: Our parents think it's a great sport. They enjoy it, too.

B *Pair work* Find out what sports your partner likes. Then write five questions about the sports. Take turns asking the questions.

4 LISTENING

CLASS
AUDIO
ONLY

 Listen to Lisa, John, Sue, and Henry talk about sports. Complete the chart.

	Favorite sport	Does he/she play or do it?	
		Yes	No
1. Lisa	*ice-skating*	☑	☐
2. John	....	☐	☐
3. Sue	....	☐	☐
4. Henry	....	☐	☐

5 CONVERSATION

TALENT SHOW
Saturday 7:00 P.M.
In the Auditorium
*Show what
you can do!*

Listen and practice.

Katherine: Oh, look. There's a talent show on Saturday. Let's enter.

Philip: I can't enter a talent show. What can I do?

Katherine: You can sing really well.

Philip: Oh! Thanks. . . . But you can, too.

Katherine: Well, no. I can't sing at all – but I can play the piano.

Philip: So maybe we *can* enter the show.

Katherine: Sure. Why not?

Philip: OK. Let's start to practice tomorrow!

6 PRONUNCIATION Can *and* can't

A Listen and practice. Notice the pronunciation of **can** and **can't**.

/kən/ /kænt/
I **can** play the guitar, but I **can't** sing very well.

B *Pair work* Do you hear **can** or **can't**? Read a sentence from the left or right column. Your partner says **can** or **can't**.

I can dance.	I can't dance.
He can swim very well.	He can't swim very well.
She can sing.	She can't sing.
They can skate very well.	They can't skate very well.

7 GRAMMAR FOCUS

Can for ability 🔊

I				you				I		
You				I				you		
He	**can**	sing very well.	**Can**	he	sing?	Yes,	he	**can**.
She	**can't**	sing at all.		she		No,	she	**can't**.
We				we				we	
They				they				they	

A Katherine is talking about things she can and can't do.
Complete these sentences. Then compare with a partner.

1. I _can_ draw.

2. I .... write poetry.

3. I .... fix cars.

4. I .... sing very well.

5. I .... play the piano.

6. I .... cook very well.

B *Pair work* Ask and answer questions about the pictures.
Respond with short answers.

A: Can Katherine draw?
B: Yes, she can.

8 LISTENING

Listen to Peter, Liz, and Scott talk about their talents.
Check (✓) the things they say they can do well.

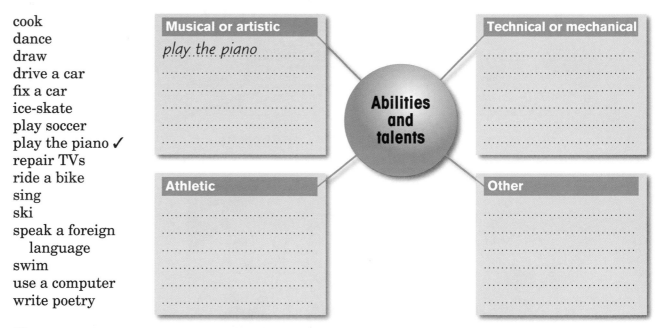

1. Peter	☐	☐	☐	☐	☐	☐	☐	☐
2. Liz	☐	☐	☐	☐	☐	☐	☐	☐
3. Scott	☐	☐	☐	☐	☐	☐	☐	☐

9 WORD POWER Abilities and talents

A Complete the word map with abilities and talents from the list.
Add two more expressions to each category.

cook
dance
draw
drive a car
fix a car
ice-skate
play soccer
play the piano ✓
repair TVs
ride a bike
sing
ski
speak a foreign
   language
swim
use a computer
write poetry

Musical or artistic
play the piano
....
....
....
....
....

Technical or mechanical
....
....
....
....
....

Abilities and talents

Athletic
....
....
....
....
....
....

Other
....
....
....
....
....
....

B *Group work* Sit in a circle. Take turns asking about the abilities
and talents in the word map.

A: Sawit, can you play the piano?
B: Yes, I can. Can you play the piano, Amara?
C: No, I can't. Can you play the piano, Somsak?

C *Class activity* Tell the class about the people in your group. Who
is musical or artistic? athletic? Who has technical or mechanical skills?
Who has other talents?

"Sawit is musical. He can play the piano and the guitar. . . ."

10 *READING*

Race the U.S.!

How many different kinds of races can you think of?

Here are three unique races:

One race takes place in a building. In the Empire State Building Run-Up, racers run up the stairs to the top of New York City's Empire State Building. The climb is 1,050 feet (320 meters) – 86 floors, or 1,575 steps. Winners can reach the top in just 10 to 11 minutes.

Racers in the Badwater Run in California run 139 miles (224 kilometers), climbing 8,653 feet (2,637 meters). The race begins in Death Valley, a desert. The temperature is about 130° F (54° C), and contestants sometimes run through sandstorms. The race ends near the top of Mount Whitney, where the temperature is only 30° F (-1° C), and there are sometimes ice storms. Amazingly, winners can usually finish in about 28 hours.

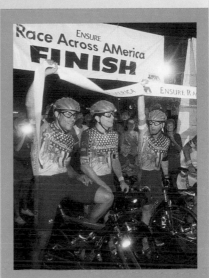

Race Across America is a bicycle race all the way across the U.S., from Irvine, California, to Savannah, Georgia. In this race, there are no "time-outs" for sleep, so the racers can sleep only about three hours each day. Winners complete the 2,900 miles (4,667 kilometers) in just eight to ten days.

A Read the article. Then complete the chart.

	Place(s)	Distance	Winning times
1. Empire State Building Run-Up	....	....	....
2. Badwater Run	....	....	....
3. Race Across America	....	....	....

B *Group work* Talk about these questions.

1. Which race is most interesting to you? Why?
2. Which race do you think is the most difficult? Why?

interchange 10

Hidden talents
Learn about your classmates' special abilities. Turn to page IC-13.

11 What are you going to do?

1 WORD POWER Dates

A  Listen. Practice the months and the ordinal numbers.

January February	March April	May June	July August	September October	November December
1st first	**2**nd second	**3**rd third	**4**th fourth	**5**th fifth	**6**th sixth	**7**th seventh
8th eighth	**9**th ninth	**10**th tenth	**11**th eleventh	**12**th twelfth	**13**th thirteenth	**14**th fourteenth
15th fifteenth	**16**th sixteenth	**17**th seventeenth	**18**th eighteenth	**19**th nineteenth	**20**th twentieth	**21**st twenty-first
22nd twenty-second	**23**rd twenty-third	**24**th twenty-fourth	**25**th twenty-fifth	**26**th twenty-sixth	**27**th twenty-seventh	**28**th twenty-eighth
29th twenty-ninth	**30**th thirtieth	**31**st thirty-first				

B *Pair work* Practice saying these dates.

1. January 1 *"January first"*
2. 6/30 *"June thirtieth"*
3. July 4
4. May 18
5. October 31
6. 2/14
7. 5/25
8. 11/2

2 CONVERSATION

A  Listen and practice.

Amy: Are you going to do anything exciting this weekend?
Philip: Well, I'm going to celebrate my birthday.
Amy: Fabulous! When is your birthday, exactly?
Philip: It's August ninth – Sunday.
Amy: So what are your plans?
Philip: Well, my friend Katherine is going to take me to a restaurant.
Amy: Nice! Is she going to order a cake?
Philip: Yeah, and the waiters are probably going to sing "Happy Birthday" to me. It's so embarrassing!

B *Class activity* Make a list of your classmates' birthdays. How many people have birthdays this week? this month? in the same month? on the same day?

A: When's your birthday?
B: July 21st. When's *your* birthday?

3 GRAMMAR FOCUS

The future with be going to 🔊

Are you **going to do** anything exciting this weekend?	Yes, I am. **I'm going to celebrate** my birthday. No, I'm not. **I'm going to stay** home.
Is Katherine **going to have** a party for you?	Yes, she is. She**'s going to invite** all my friends. No, she isn't. She**'s going to take** me out to a restaurant.
Are the waiters **going to sing** to you?	Yes, they are. They**'re going to sing** "Happy Birthday." No, they aren't. But they**'re going to give** me a cake.

A Are you going to do any of these things this weekend? Write ten sentences. Then compare with a partner.

Things I'm going to do this weekend	*Things I'm not going to do this weekend*
I'm going to see friends.	*I'm not going to watch TV.*

B *Pair work* Ask questions about your partner's plans for the weekend.

A: Are you going to see a movie this weekend?
B: Yes, I am. I'm going to see the new Tom Cruise movie.
A: Are you going to go with a friend? . . .

4 PRONUNCIATION *Reduction of* going to

A Listen and practice. **Going to** is sometimes pronounced /gənə/ in conversation.

A: Are you **going to** have a party for your birthday?
B: No, I'm **going to** go out with a friend.

A: Are you **going to** go to a restaurant?
B: Yes. We're **going to** go to Nick's Café.

B Ask another classmate about weekend plans. Try to reduce **going to** to /gənə/.

5 LISTENING

A It's five-thirty in the evening, and these people are waiting for the bus. What are their plans for tonight? Write one guess for each person.

CLASS AUDIO ONLY ▶

B  Listen to the people talk about their evening plans. What are they really going to do? Complete the chart.

Michelle   Kevin   Robert   Jane

Your guess	What they're really going to do
Michelle *is going to go to the gym.*	Michelle
Kevin	Kevin
Robert	Robert
Jane	Jane

6 SNAPSHOT

Do you know these holidays in the United States?

New Year's Day January 1	Valentine's Day February 14	Independence Day July 4	Halloween October 31	Thanksgiving 4th Thursday in November	Christmas December 25

Do you celebrate any similar holidays? How?
What are some holidays in your country? What's your favorite holiday? Why?

7 CONVERSATION

 Listen and practice.

Monica: So, Dennis. What are you going to do for Thanksgiving?
Dennis: I'm going to have dinner at my parents' house. What about you? Any plans?
Monica: Yeah. I'm going to cook dinner with some friends. We're going to make fish soup.
Dennis: Hmm. That's unusual. We always have turkey, mashed potatoes . . . .
Monica: I know. Every year, my friends and I make something different.
Dennis: Sounds like fun. Well, have a happy Thanksgiving.
Monica: Thanks. You, too.

8 GRAMMAR FOCUS

Wh-questions with be going to 🔊	

Where are you going to go for the holiday?
   We're going to go to my parents' house.
Who's going to be there?
   My whole family is going to be there.
How are you going to get there?
   We're going to drive.
	Time expressions
	tonight
	tomorrow
	tomorrow night
	next week
	next month
	next summer

Complete this conversation with the correct verb forms.
Then practice with a partner.

A: What _are_ you _going to do_ for Halloween? (do)
B: I don't know. I .... anything special. (not do)
A: Well, Pat and I .... a party. Can you come? (have)
B: Sure, I can come. Where .... you .... the party? (have)
A: It .... at Pat's house. (be)
B: What time .... the party .... ? (start)
A: At 6:00. And it .... around midnight. (end)
B: Who .... you .... ? (invite)
A: We .... all our good friends. (ask)

9 EVERYDAY EVENTS

Group work Ask and answer questions about your plans for . . . .

tomorrow night
Saturday night
next week
this/next summer

A: What are you going to do tomorrow night?
B: I'm going to stay home and watch television. What about you? What are you going to do?
C: I'm going to . . . .

10 HOLIDAYS

A *Pair work* Choose a holiday or celebration. Then ask and answer these questions with a partner. Use the activities in the box or your own ideas.

What holiday are you thinking about?
What are you going to do?
Where are you going to go?
Who's going to be there?
When are you going to go?
How are you going to get there?

Some activities
see friends
have a party/picnic
make dinner
go to a parade
open presents

A: What holiday are you thinking about?
B: I'm thinking about Lunar New Year.
A: What are you going to do for Lunar New Year?
B: I'm going to go to a parade with my brother. . . .

B *Class activity* Tell the class about your partner's plans for the holiday.

interchange 11

Celebrations

Talk about how people are celebrating special events. Turn to page IC-14.

11 *READING*

WHAT ARE YOU GOING TO DO ON YOUR BIRTHDAY?

How do people usually celebrate birthdays in your country?

Elena Buenaventura
Madrid
"My twenty-first birthday is on Saturday, and I'm going to go out with some friends. To wish me a happy birthday, they're going to pull on my ear 21 times, once for each year. It's an old custom. Some people pull on the ear just once, but my friends are very traditional!"

Yan-Ching Shi
Taipei
"Tomorrow is my sixteenth birthday. It's a special birthday, so we're going to have a family ceremony. I'm probably going to get some money in 'lucky' envelopes from my relatives. My mother is going to cook noodles – noodles are for a long life."

Mr. and Mrs. Aoki
Kyoto
"My husband is going to be 60 tomorrow. In Japan, the sixtieth birthday is called *kanreki* – it's the beginning of a new life. The color red represents a new life, so we always give something red for a sixtieth birthday. What am I going to give my husband? I can't say. It's a surprise!"

Philippe Joly
Paris
"I'm going to be 30 next week, so I'm going to invite three very good friends out to dinner. In France, when you have a birthday, you often invite people out. In some countries, I know it's the opposite – people take you out."

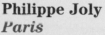

A Read the four paragraphs. Then correct these statements.

1. To celebrate her birthday, Elena is going to pull on her friends' ears.
2. Yan-Ching is going to cook some noodles on her birthday.
3. On his birthday, Mr. Aoki is going to buy something red.
4. Philippe's friends are going to take him out to dinner on his birthday.

B *Group work* What do you usually do on your birthday? Do you have plans for your next birthday, or for the birthday of a friend or family member? What are you going to do? Tell the group.

"I'm going to be 25 on March 15th. I'm going to . . . ."

12 What's the matter?

1 WORD POWER Parts of the body

A  Listen and practice.

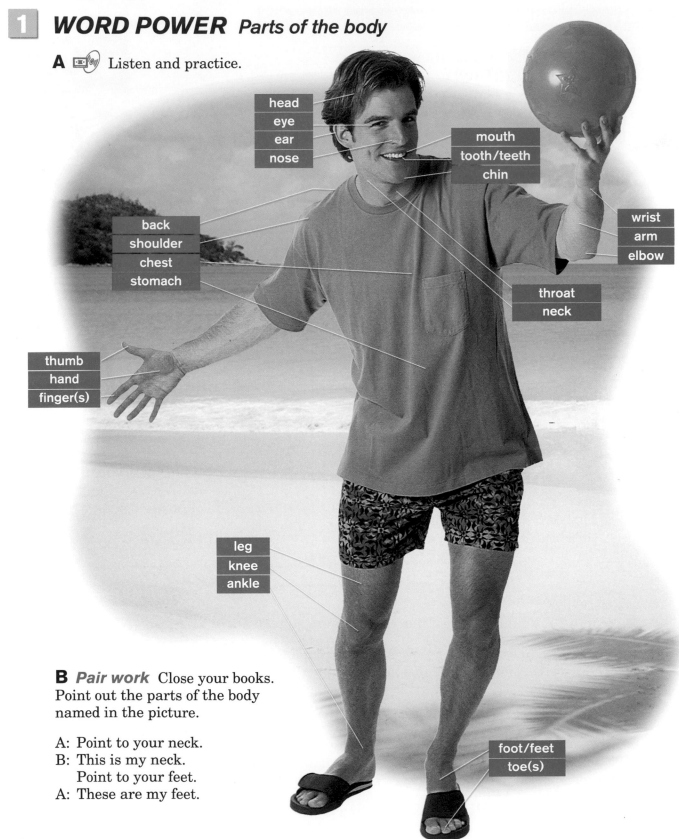

head
eye
ear
nose

mouth
tooth/teeth
chin

wrist
arm
elbow

back
shoulder
chest
stomach

throat
neck

thumb
hand
finger(s)

leg
knee
ankle

foot/feet
toe(s)

B *Pair work* Close your books.
Point out the parts of the body
named in the picture.

A: Point to your neck.
B: This is my neck.
   Point to your feet.
A: These are my feet.

2 CONVERSATION

🎧 Listen and practice.

Brian: Hey, Ken. How are you?
  Ken: Oh, I'm not so good, actually.
Brian: Why? What's the matter?
  Ken: Well, I have a headache. And a backache.
Brian: Maybe you have the flu.
  Ken: No, I think I just miss Japan – I feel a little homesick.
Brian: That's too bad. . . . But I think I can help. Let's have lunch at that new Japanese restaurant.
  Ken: That's a great idea. Thanks, Brian. I feel better already!

3 GRAMMAR FOCUS

Have + *noun;* feel + *adjective* 🎧

What's the matter?
What's wrong?
  I have a headache.
  I have a sore throat.
  I have the flu.
	How do you feel?
	  I feel sick.
	  I feel sad.
	  I feel better.
	  I don't feel well.
		Adjectives	–
			 sick
			 sad
			 bad
			 awful
			 terrible
				+
				 fine (well)
				 happy
				 good (better)
				 great
				 terrific

A 🎧 Listen and practice. *"He has a backache."*

  a backache   an earache   a headache   a stomachache   a toothache

  a cold   a cough   a fever   the flu   sore eyes   a sore throat

B *Pair work* Take turns acting out a health problem. Your partner guesses the problem and gives sympathy.

A: What's wrong? Do you have a headache?
B: No, I don't.
A: Do you have an earache?

B: Yes, I have an earache.
A: That's too bad.

73

C *Group work* Find out how your classmates feel today.

A: How do you feel today?
B: I feel fine, thanks. What about you?
A: I feel really terrible. I have a headache.
B: I'm sorry to hear that. How do you feel today, Sun-hee?
C: . . .

expressions
That's too bad. I'm sorry to hear that. I hope you feel better soon.

4 LISTENING *Health problems*

Listen to people talk about health problems. Where do they have problems? Write down the parts of the body. Then ask and answer questions.

1. Ben *head, throat* …… 2. Alison …… 3. Jeffrey …… 4. Marta ……

A: What's wrong with Ben?
B: He has a headache and a sore throat.

5 SNAPSHOT

 Listen and practice.

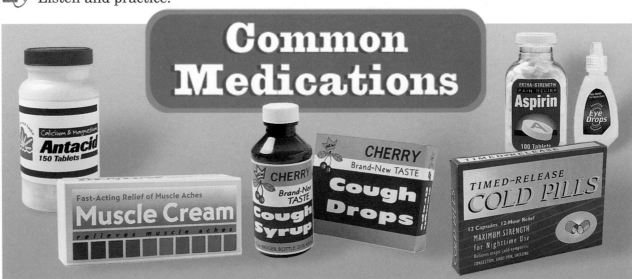

Sources: Adapted from *Almanac of the American People* and interviews with adults between 25 and 50

What can you use these medications for?
What medications do you have at home? Which do you use often?

6 CONVERSATION

 Listen and practice.

Dr. Young: Hello, Ms. West. How are you today?
Ms. West: I feel terrible.
Dr. Young: So, what's wrong, exactly?
Ms. West: I'm exhausted.
Dr. Young: Hmm. Why are you so tired?
Ms. West: I just can't sleep at night.
Dr. Young: OK. Let's take a look at you.

Dr. Young: I'm going to give you some pills.
Take one pill every night after dinner.
Ms. West: OK.
Dr. Young: And don't drink coffee, tea, or soda.
Ms. West: No soda?
Dr. Young: No. And don't work too hard.
Ms. West: All right. Thanks, Dr. Young.

7 LISTENING

  Listen to Dr. Young talk to four other patients. What does she give them? Check (✓) the correct medication.

	Antacid	Aspirin	Cold pills	Eyedrops	Muscle cream
1. Ben	☐	☐	☐	☐	☐
2. Alison	☐	☐	☐	☐	☐
3. Jeffrey	☐	☐	☐	☐	☐
4. Marta	☐	☐	☐	☐	☐

8 PRONUNCIATION *Sentence stress*

A Listen and practice. Notice the main stress in these sentences.

Take some áspirin.   Don't drink cóffee.
Go to béd.   Don't go to wórk.
Use some múscle cream.   Don't éxercise this week.

B Listen and mark the main stress in these sentences.

Take a hot bath.   Stay in bed.   Don't lift heavy things.

Don't drink soda.   Eat a lot of vegetables.   Don't go to bed late.

9 GRAMMAR FOCUS

Imperatives 📻

Take a pill every four hours.	**Don't work** too hard.
Drink lots of juice.	**Don't stay up** late.

A What are these people saying? Choose from the sentences in the box. Then compare with a partner.

I can't sleep at night.
I have the flu.
I can't lose weight.
✓ I have a stomachache.
I'm homesick.
My job is very stressful.
There's no food in the house.

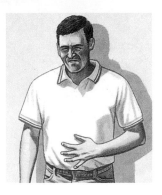 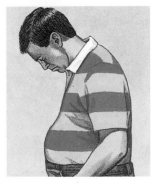 

1. *I have a stomachache.* 2. .... 3. ....

4. .... 5. .... 6. .... 7. ....

B *Pair work* Act out the problems in part A and give advice. Use these or your own ideas.

Go to bed and sleep.	Go out to a restaurant.	Eat some toast and drink some tea.
Don't go to school this week.	Don't go outside.	Don't eat desserts.
Don't eat any heavy food today.	Take two aspirin.	Close your eyes for ten minutes.
Go home and relax.	Do something fun every evening.	Call your family on the phone.
Get some exercise every day.	Go to a store and buy some food.	

A: I have a stomachache.
B: Don't eat any heavy food today.

10 READING

10 SIMPLE WAYS TO IMPROVE YOUR HEALTH

Cover the reading. Can you think of some ways to improve your health?

Believe it or not, you can greatly improve your health in these ten simple ways:

1
Eat breakfast. Breakfast gives you energy for the morning.

2
Go for a walk. Walking is good exercise, and exercise is necessary for good health.

3
Floss your teeth. Don't just brush them. Flossing keeps your gums healthy.

4
Drink eight cups of water every day. Water helps your body in many ways.

5
Stretch for five minutes. Stretching is important for your muscles.

6
Wear a seat belt. Every year, seat belts save thousands of lives.

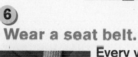

7
Do something to challenge your brain. For example, do a crossword puzzle or read a new book.

8
Moisturize your skin and use sunscreen.

9
Get enough calcium. Your bones need it. Yogurt and milk have calcium. Or drink orange juice with calcium added.

10
Take a "time-out" – a break of about 20 minutes. Do something different. For example, get up and walk. Or sit down and listen to music.

Source: *Cooking Light* ® Magazine

A Read the article. Then complete the advice.

1. To get exercise, ...
2. To help your bones, ...
3. To help your muscles, ...
4. To keep your gums healthy, ...
5. To have enough energy for the morning, ...
6. To challenge your brain, ...

B *Group work* Talk about these questions.

1. Which of these ten things do you do regularly?
2. What else do you do for your health?

interchange 12

Helpful advice
Give advice for some common problems.
Turn to page IC-15.

Review of Units 9-12

1 MEALTIME

A Complete the chart.

	Breakfast	Lunch	Dinner
1. What time do you usually eat?	....	....	....
2. Where do you usually eat?	....	....	....
3. What do you usually have?	....	....	....
	....	....	....

B *Pair work* Take turns. Ask and answer the questions.

2 LISTENING *What's the matter?*

 CLASS AUDIO ONLY

Listen to these conversations. Match the conversations with the problems.

1. ..*d*.. 2. .... 3. .... 4. .... 5. .... 6. ....

a. This person needs some ketchup.

b. This person has a backache.

c. This person can't dance very well.

d. This person feels sad.

e. This person is going to take a test tomorrow.

f. This person has the flu.

3 LIKE IT OR NOT?

A Complete the chart with one item in each category.

	Food	Sports	Music
Love	....	....	....
Like	....	....	....
Hate	....	....	....

B *Pair work* Compare your information.

A: What food do you love?
B: I love bananas. How about you?
    What do you think of bananas?
A: I hate bananas, but I love ice cream.

4 PLANS, PLANS, PLANS

A Write answers to these questions. Then write three more questions.

1. Where are you going to go after class today?
2. How are you going to get home today?
3. Who's going to make your dinner this evening?
4. Who are you going to eat dinner with?
5. What are you going to do tonight?
6. What time are you going to go to bed tonight?
7. What are you going to do this weekend?
8. ....
9. ....
10. ....

B *Group work* Take turns. Ask and answer the questions.

5 LISTENING

CLASS AUDIO ONLY

Some people are planning a barbecue. Listen to the questions. Check (✓) the correct response.

1. ☑ No. They have the flu.
   ☐ No, she isn't.

2. ☐ Yes, you can go.
   ☐ Yes. Let's get some paper.

3. ☐ Yes. Buy some.
   ☐ No, there aren't any.

4. ☐ No, I'm not.
   ☐ No, I don't.

5. ☐ No. We need some.
   ☐ No, we aren't.

6. ☐ No. I like chocolate cake.
   ☐ No, we don't have any.

13 You can't miss it.

1 WORD POWER Places and things

A Where can you buy these things?
Match the items with the places.
Then listen and practice.
"You can buy aspirin at a drugstore."

1. aspirin ..*b*..

2. traveler's
   checks ......

3. bread ......

4. a sandwich ......

5. a dictionary ......

6. stamps ......

7. gasoline ......

8. a sweatshirt ......

a. a bank

b. a drugstore

c. a bookstore

d. a gas station

e. a restaurant

f. a post office

g. a department store

h. a supermarket

B *Pair work* What else can you buy or do in these places? Make a list.

A: You can buy cough drops at a drugstore.
B: You can buy cold pills at a drugstore, too.

80

2 LISTENING

CLASS
AUDIO
ONLY

A Listen to the Andersons talk about shopping. What do they need? Where are they going to buy these things? Complete the chart.

	What	Where
1. Sarah	a swimsuit	
2. Mom		the supermarket
3. Dad		
4. Mike		

B *Pair work* What shopping plans do you have this week? Tell your partner.

"I'm going to go to a bookstore. I need to buy . . . ."

3 CONVERSATION

Listen and practice.

Don: Excuse me. Can you help me? Is there a public rest room around here?
Woman: A public rest room? Hmm. I'm sorry. I don't think so.
Don: Oh, no. My son needs a bathroom.
Woman: Well, there's a department store on Main Street.
Don: Where on Main Street?
Woman: It's on the corner of Main and First Avenue.
Don: On the corner of Main and First?
Woman: Yes. It's across from the park. You can't miss it.
Don: Thanks a lot!

4 PRONUNCIATION *Checking information*

Listen and practice. To check information, repeat the information as a question. Use rising intonation.

1. A: The department store is on the corner of Main and First Avenue.

B: **On the corner of Main and First?**
A: Yes. It's across from the park.

2. A: There's a coffee shop next to the shoe store.

B: **Next to the shoe store?**
A: Yes. You can't miss it.

5 GRAMMAR FOCUS

Prepositions of place

on	on the corner of	across from	next to	between

There's a department store **on** Main Street.
It's **on the corner of** Main and First.
It's **across from** the park.

It's **next to** the bank.
The bank is **on** Main Street,
   between First and Second Avenues.

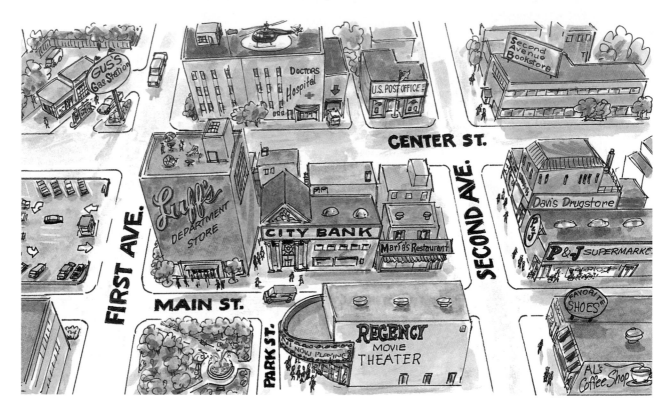

A Look at the map and complete these sentences. Then compare with a partner.

1. Al's Coffee Shop is ......*on*...... Second Avenue, ...*next to*..... the shoe store.
2. The Regency Movie Theater is .... Park Street, ... the park.
3. There's a bank .... the department store.
4. There's a drugstore .... Second Avenue. It's .... Main and Center.
5. There's a gas station .... First Avenue and Center Street.

B *Pair work* Write three sentences about other places on the map.
Read your sentences to your partner. Your partner guesses the places.

A: It's on Main Street, across from the restaurant.
B: Is it the movie theater?
A: Yes, it is.

6 LISTENING

CLASS AUDIO ONLY ▶ Look at the map in Exercise 5. Listen to four conversations. Where are the people going?

1. *City Bank* .... 2. .... 3. .... 4. ....

7 SNAPSHOT

 The Golden Gate Bridge

 The Museum of Science and Industry

 The White House

 THE STATUE OF LIBERTY

Source: Adapted from *Fodor's USA*

Do you know where these places are? (Check your answers in the appendix.)
Do you know any other tourist attractions in the United States?
What are some popular attractions in your country?

8 CONVERSATION

Listen and practice.

Tourist: Excuse me, ma'am. Can you help me? How do I get to St. Patrick's Cathedral?
Woman: Just walk up Fifth Avenue to 50th Street. St. Patrick's is on the right.
Tourist: Is it near Rockefeller Center?
Woman: It's right across from Rockefeller Center.
Tourist: Thank you. And where is the Empire State Building? Is it far from here?
Woman: It's right behind you. Just turn around and look up!

9 GRAMMAR FOCUS

Giving directions 🔈

How do I get to Rockefeller Center?
Walk up/Go up Fifth Avenue **to** 49th Street.
Turn left at 49th Street.
It's **on the right**.

How do I get to Bryant Park?
Walk down/Go down Fifth Avenue **for** eight blocks.
Turn right at 42nd Street.
It's **on the left**.

Pair work Look at the map.
Take turns giving directions.

1 You're at the Empire State Building.
You're going to Rockefeller Center.

A: How do I get to Rockefeller Center?
B: Walk up . . . .

2 You're at Rockefeller Center. You're going to the New York Public Library.

3 You're at St. Patrick's Cathedral. You're going to the Empire State Building.

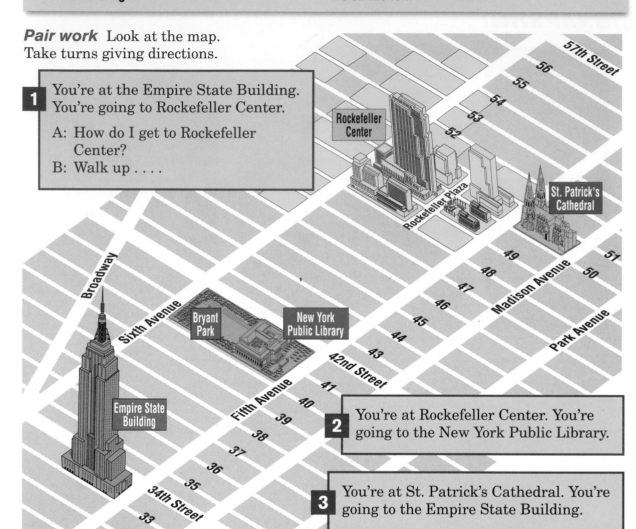

10 AROUND TOWN

Group work Choose an area of your city and draw a street map. Then take turns asking for and giving directions to places on your map.

A: Excuse me. Is there a bookstore near here?
B: Yes, there is. It's on California Avenue, across from Hannah's Restaurant.
A: How do I get there?
B: Walk . . . .

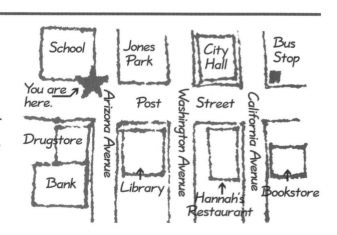

11 READING

⏏A walk up FIFTH Avenue

As you read, look at the map on page 84.

1 Start your tour at the **Empire State Building** on Fifth Avenue between 33rd and 34th Streets. This building has 102 floors. Take the elevator to the 102nd floor for a great view of New York City.

2 Now walk up Fifth Avenue seven blocks to the **New York Public Library**. The entrance is between 40th and 42nd Streets. This library holds over 10 million books. Behind the library is **Bryant Park**. In the summer, there's an outdoor café, and at lunch hour, there are free music concerts.

3 Walk up Sixth Avenue to 49th Street. You're standing in the middle of the 19 buildings of **Rockefeller Center**. Turn right on 49th Street, walk another block, and turn left. You're in Rockefeller Plaza. In the winter, you can ice-skate in the rink there.

4 Right across from Rockefeller Center on Fifth Avenue is **St. Patrick's Cathedral**. It's modeled after the cathedral in Cologne, Germany. Go inside St. Patrick's and leave the noisy city behind. Look at the beautiful blue windows. Many of these windows come from France.

A Read the article. Where can you . . . ?

1. have a view of the city ....
2. go ice-skating in the winter ....
3. listen to music outdoors ....
4. sit quietly indoors ....

B *Group work* Ask the questions in part A. Answer using information about your hometown.

A: Where can you listen to music outdoors?
B: You can listen to music in the park next to the river.
C: Or you can . . . .

interchange 13

Directions
Find your way around. Student A turns to page IC-16. Student B turns to page IC-18.

14 Did you have a good weekend?

Some Common Chores

shop for groceries

clean the house

vacuum and dust

work in the yard

pay bills

do the laundry

Which of these chores do you do on weekends?
What other chores do you do?
What else do you do on weekends?

2 **CONVERSATION**

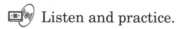 Listen and practice.

Michael: Did you have a good weekend?
Jennifer: Yes, I did. But I feel a little
tired today.
Michael: Really? Why?
Jennifer: Well, on Saturday, I exercised in
the morning. Then my roommate
and I cleaned and shopped. And
then I visited my parents.
Michael: So what did you do on Sunday?
Jennifer: I studied for the test all day.
Michael: Oh, no! Do we have a test today?
I didn't study! I just watched TV
all weekend!

3 GRAMMAR FOCUS

Simple past statements: regular verbs

							Spelling
I	**studied**	on Sunday.	I	**didn't study**	on Saturday.		watch → watch**ed**
You	**watched**	TV all weekend.	You	**didn't watch**	TV during the week.		exercise → exercise**d**
She	**stayed**	home on Sunday.	She	**didn't stay**	home on Saturday.		study → stud**ied**
We	**visited**	my parents.	We	**didn't visit**	any friends.		stay → stay**ed**
You	**shopped**	for groceries.	You	**didn't shop**	for clothes.		shop → shop**ped**
They	**exercised**	on Saturday.	They	**didn't exercise**	on Sunday.		

didn't = did not

Complete these sentences with the correct verb forms.
Then compare with a partner.

What did you do this weekend?

1. I *waited.* (wait) for a phone call, but my girlfriend
   didn't call. (not call).

2. I .... (stay) home and .... (watch) TV.

3. My friend Frank .... (visit) me. We .... (talk)
   and .... (listen) to music.

4. We .... (invite) some friends over,
   and we .... (cook) a great meal.

5. I .... (study) on Saturday, but I ....
   (not work) on Sunday. I .... (walk) to the mall
   and .... (shop) all day.

4 PRONUNCIATION   Regular simple past verbs

A Listen and practice. Notice the pronunciation of
simple past endings.

/t/	/d/	/ɪd/
work**ed**	clean**ed**	invit**ed**
watch**ed**	stay**ed**	visit**ed**
....	....	....
....	....	....
....	....	....
....	....	....

B Listen and write these verbs under the correct sounds.

asked	cooked	listened	rented	studied	walked
called	exercised	needed	shopped	waited	wanted

5 DID YOU OR DIDN'T YOU?

Pair work Write about four things you did and four things you didn't do last weekend. Use these or other expressions. Then tell your partner about your weekend.

listen to music

work in the yard

wash my clothes

relax

rent a video

invite friends to my house

cook a meal

visit my family

Things I did last weekend	Things I didn't do last weekend
I listened to music.	I didn't work in the yard.

A: I listened to music last weekend.
B: I listened to music, too. I didn't work in the yard.
A: I didn't work in the yard, either.

6 WORD POWER *Irregular simple past verbs*

A Listen and practice. Notice the irregular simple past forms.

> I **slept** late on Saturday. I **got up** at ten, **read** the newspaper, and **ate** breakfast.

> We **saw** a movie. We **bought** popcorn, **drank** some soda, and **had** a lot of fun!

> I **met** a friend at the park and **went** jogging. Then I **came** home and **felt** really tired.

B Complete the chart. Then compare with a partner.

Present	Past	Present	Past	Present	Past
buy	bought	....	felt	....	met
....	came	....	got up	....	read /rɛd/
....	drank	....	went	....	saw
....	ate	....	had	....	slept

For a list of more irregular past forms, see the appendix.

7 CONVERSATION

🔊 Listen and practice.

Laura: So, did you go out with Sam?
Erica: Yes, I did. We went out on Saturday night.
We saw the new Leonardo DiCaprio movie.
Laura: Did you like it?
Erica: I liked it a lot, but Sam didn't.
Laura: Oh, well. Did you do anything else?
Erica: Yeah. We went to a dance club.
Laura: Did you have fun?
Erica: Yes, we did. We had a great time. And
we're going to go out again next weekend.

8 GRAMMAR FOCUS

Simple past yes/no questions 🔊

Did you **go** out this weekend?	**Did** you **have** a good time?
Yes, I **did**. I **went** to the movies.	No, I **didn't**. I **had** a terrible time.

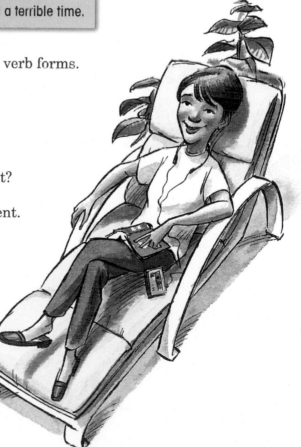

A Complete these conversations with the correct verb forms.
Then practice with a partner.

1. A: ...*Did*... you ..*have*.. (have) a good weekend?
   B: Yes, I .... I .... (have) a
   great weekend. I just relaxed.

2. A: .... you .... (eat out) on Friday night?
   B: No, I .... Some friends .... (come)
   over. We .... (eat) dinner at my apartment.
   Then we .... (go) to a movie.

3. A: .... you .... (read) the newspaper
   this morning?
   B: Yes, I .... I .... (read) it at work.

4. A: .... you .... (have) breakfast
   this morning?
   B: No, I .... I .... (get up) late.
   But I .... (buy) a cup of coffee
   and .... (drink) it on the bus.

B *Pair work* Take turns asking the questions
in part A. Answer with your own information.

89

9 LISTENING

   Listen to Andy, Mark, Patrick, and Matt talk about their weekends. What did they do on Saturday morning? Write their names under the pictures.

 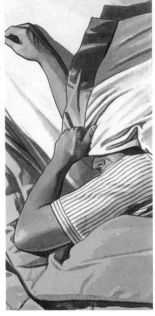  

....

10 YOUR WEEKEND

A *Pair work* Check (✓) seven questions to ask your partner about last weekend. Then take turns asking and answering questions.

☐ Did you read any books last weekend?	☐ Did you have dinner at a restaurant?
☐ Did you write any letters?	☐ Did you see any movies?
☐ Did you work around the house?	☐ Did you go dancing?
☐ Did you exercise or play any sports?	☐ Did you meet any interesting people?
☐ Did you go shopping?	☐ Did you talk on the phone?
☐ Did you buy any clothes?	☐ Did you sleep late?
☐ Did you see any friends?	☐ Did you study?

A: Did you read any books last weekend?
B: Yes, I did. I finished John Grisham's new book.
   I loved it! Did you go shopping?
A: No, I didn't. I didn't have any money.

B *Class activity* Tell the class about your partner's weekend.

"Maria read John Grisham's new book. She loved it. . . ."

interchange 14

Past and present
Are you different now
from when you were
a child?
Turn to page IC-17.

11 *READING*

THE CHANGING WEEKEND

What do you think Americans in the early twentieth century (1900–1925) did on weekends? What do they do on weekends now?

THEN

Once upon a time, people spent lots of time at home on weekends. Then, new inventions changed the weekend.

● People used electric streetcars to travel in cities. On weekends, they rode the streetcars to amusement parks. Young people liked roller coasters and the Ferris wheel.

● The first movies lasted only one minute. Soon, however, movies got longer. By the 1920s, movie theaters sold millions of tickets each week! In 1927, movies finally had sound. Sometimes, people stayed home instead, and listened to another new invention – the radio.

● People in cities worked indoors during the week, so they wanted to be outdoors on weekends. Bicycling became a popular activity.

NOW

With more time, money, and inventions, people have many more choices.

● They can visit huge "theme parks" like Disney World and ride modern roller coasters that go higher and faster than ever before.

● They can choose from lots of different movies at a multiplex (a building with many movie theaters) or watch a video at home.

● Many people jog, bicycle, work out at the gym, or play sports. Others turn on their TV and watch sports.

A Read the article. Then read a passage from a man's diary from 1925. Based on the article, some of the things he writes about are not possible. Rewrite the passage with information that is possible.

> Monday, June 8, 1925
>   amusement
> (1) Betty and I took a streetcar to the ~~theme~~ park on Saturday. (2) We rode on the Ferris wheel and the roller coaster. (3) On Saturday night, I took Betty to a movie at the multiplex. (4) The movie had really interesting sound effects. (5) On Sunday afternoon, I bicycled with my sister. (6) By Sunday night, I felt pretty tired, so I stayed home and watched TV.

B *Group work* Talk about this question.

Do you think the weekend changed a lot from the early twentieth century to now in your country? Explain.

15 Where were you born?

1 SNAPSHOT

Famous Americans Born in Other Places

John Leguizamo

*Born in Colombia in 1964
*TV, theater, and film actor
*Playwright

Carolina Herrera

*Born in Venezuela in 1939
*Fashion designer
*Founder of an
 internationally known
 fashion-design house

Midori

*Born in Japan in 1971
*Concert violinist
*Founder of an organization
 to promote music education

Jerry Yang

*Born in Taiwan in 1968
*Co-founder of Yahoo! Inc.,
 the first directory to the
 Internet's World Wide Web

Are there famous people in your country from other places? Who?
Do you have friends or relatives from other countries? Where are they from?

2 CONVERSATION

 Listen and practice.

Chuck: Where were you born, Melissa?
Melissa: I was born in Korea.
Chuck: Oh! So you weren't born in the U.S.
Melissa: No. I came here in 1995.
Chuck: Hmm. You were pretty young.
Melissa: Well, I was seventeen.
Chuck: Did you go to college right away?
Melissa: No. My English wasn't very good,
 so I took English classes for
 two years first.
Chuck: Your English is really
 fluent now.
Melissa: Thanks. Your English
 is pretty good, too!
Chuck: Yeah, but I was born here!

3 GRAMMAR FOCUS

Statements with the past of be 🔊

I	**was**	born in Korea.	I	**wasn't**	born in the U.S.	**wasn't = was not**
You	**were**	pretty young.	You	**weren't**	very old.	**weren't = were not**
She	**was**	seventeen.	She	**wasn't**	in college.	
We	**were**	born the same year.	We	**weren't**	born in the same country.	
They	**were**	in Korea in 1994.	They	**weren't**	in the U.S. in 1994.	

A Melissa is talking about her family. Choose the correct verb form. Then compare with a partner.

Seoul

My family and I ...*were*.. (was/were) all born

in Korea – we .... (wasn't/weren't) born in the U.S.

I .... (was/were) born in the city of Inchon,

and my brother .... (was/were) born there, too.

My parents .... (wasn't/weren't) born in Inchon.

They .... (was/were) born in the capital, Seoul.

Questions with the past of be 🔊

When	were	you born?	I **was** born in 1978.	
	Were	you born in the U.S.?	No, I **wasn't**.	
Where	were	you born?	I **was** born in Korea.	
	Was	your brother born in Korea?	Yes, he **was**.	
What city	was	he born in?	He **was** born in Inchon.	
	Were	your parents born in Inchon?	No, they **weren't**.	
Where	were	they born?	They **were** born in Seoul.	

B Complete these questions with **was** or **were**. Then ask and answer the questions with a partner.

1. ..*Were*.. you born in this city?
2. When .... you born?
3. Where .... your parents born?
4. When .... your mother born?
5. When .... your father born?
6. .... you and your family in this city last year?
7. .... you at this school last year?
8. Who .... your first English teacher?
9. What nationality .... your first English teacher?
10. What .... he or she like?

Years 🔊
1906 (nineteen oh six)
1917 (nineteen seventeen)
1999 (nineteen ninety-nine)
2000 (two thousand)

A: Were you born in this city?
B: No, I wasn't. I was born in Istanbul.

4 LISTENING

Where were these people born? When were they born?
Listen and complete the chart.

	Place of birth	Year of birth
1. Michelle Yeoh	....	....
2. Masahiko Harada	....	....
3. Helena Bonham Carter	....	....
4. Gustavo Kuerten	....	....

5 PRONUNCIATION *Negative contractions*

A Listen and practice.

one syllable	*two syllables*
aren't	isn't
weren't	wasn't
don't	doesn't
	didn't

B Listen and practice.

She **didn't** call because there **wasn't** time.
They **aren't** there, but she **doesn't** know.
They **don't** go out often, but they **aren't** home today.
She **isn't** going to wait because she **doesn't** have time.
They **weren't** home yesterday, either.

6 CONVERSATION

🔊 Listen and practice.

Melissa: Where did you grow up, Chuck?
Chuck: I grew up in Texas. I was born there, too.
Melissa: And when did you come to Los Angeles?
Chuck: In 1985. I went to college here.
Melissa: Oh. What was your major?
Chuck: Drama. I was an actor for five years after college.
Melissa: That's interesting. So why did you become a hairstylist?
Chuck: Because I needed the money. And I love it. Look. What do you think?

7 GRAMMAR FOCUS

Wh-questions with did, was, *and* were 🔊			
Where did you grow up?	I **grew up** in Texas.	**How old were you** in 1985?	I **was** eighteen.
When did you come to L.A.?	I **came** to L.A. in 1985.	**What was your major** in college?	It **was** drama.
Why did you become a hairstylist?	Because I **needed** the money.	**How was college?**	It **was** great.

A Match the questions with the answers. Then compare with a partner.

1. When and where were you born? ...c...
2. Where did you grow up? ....
3. When did you start school? ....
4. How old were you then? ....
5. How was your first day of school? ....
6. Who was your first friend in school? ....
7. What was he/she like? ....
8. Why did you take this class? ....

a. I was six.
b. She was really shy.
c. I was born in 1978 in Puebla, Mexico.
d. Her name was Margarita.
e. My English wasn't very good.
f. I grew up in Mexico City.
g. I entered first grade in 1984.
h. It was a little scary.

B *Pair work* Take turns asking the questions in part A.
Answer with your own information.

8 LAST SATURDAY

Group work Take turns. Ask and answer questions about last
Saturday. Use these questions and your own ideas.

Where were you last Saturday?   Where were you in the evening? Were you alone?
Who was with you?   When did you have dinner?
What did you do?   What did you eat? Was the food good?
Where did you have lunch?   What time did you go to bed?
What did you do in the afternoon?   Were you very tired Saturday night?

A: Where were you last Saturday?
B: I was at home.
C: Who was with you?
B: My mother and brother were at home, too.
   My father was at work.
D: What did you . . . ?

9 WORD POWER School subjects

A Complete the chart with words from the list. Then compare with a partner.

algebra ✓
art
biology
calculus
chemistry
Chinese
computer science
drama
French
geometry
history
journalism
music
physical education
physics
psychology
sociology
Spanish

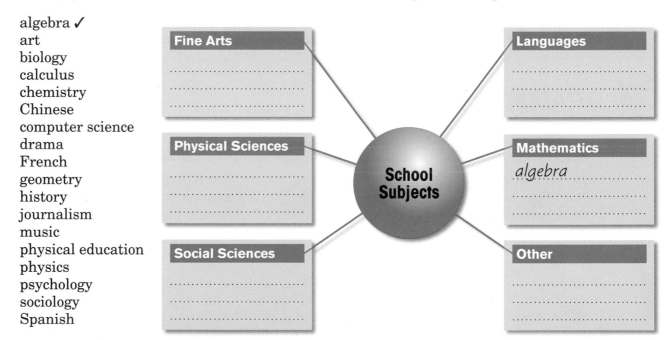

Fine Arts

Languages

Physical Sciences

School
Subjects

Mathematics
algebra

Social Sciences

Other

B **Pair work** Choose a column. Then take turns asking
and answering the questions.

You're in high school now.	You're not in high school now.
What classes did you take last year?	What classes did you take in high school?
What was your favorite class?	What were your favorite subjects?
What classes didn't you like?	Which subjects didn't you like?
Who was your favorite teacher? Why?	Who was your favorite teacher? Why?

10 READING

 # Three Famous Artists

The article is about a printmaker, a painter, and a sculptor. Look at the artists' names, when they lived, and where they were born. Can you match each work of art with the artist?

Hiroshige (1797–1858)

Hiroshige was born in Edo (now Tokyo). As a boy, he studied with a famous artist. Hiroshige traveled to many beautiful places in Japan. His woodblock prints are landscapes – mountains, fields, rivers – with small human figures. Hiroshige's prints suggest strong feelings about these places.

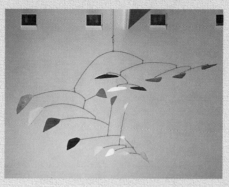

1. ....

2. ....

Frida Kahlo (1907–1954)

Frida Kahlo was born near Mexico City. At 15, she almost died in a bus accident. For the rest of her life, she was disabled and in pain. Soon after the accident, Kahlo taught herself how to paint. Kahlo is especially famous for her self-portraits. In these paintings, Kahlo used bright colors and strange symbols to show her feelings.

Alexander Calder (1898–1976)

Alexander Calder was born in Philadelphia. First, he studied engineering. At the age of 25, he went to art school. Calder developed a new kind of sculpture: the mobile. Mobiles hang from the ceiling and move in interesting patterns. In many of Calder's mobiles, wires connect flat, colorful metal shapes.

3. ....

A Read the article. Then write a question with **What**, **Where**, or **When**. Include the artist's name in the question.

1. *What is Hiroshige famous for?*   For beautiful landscapes.
2. .... In Philadelphia.
3. .... In 1797.
4. .... Near Mexico City.
5. .... In 1898.
6. .... For self-portraits.

interchange 15
Time line
Map out the most important events in your life. Turn to page IC-20.

B Group work Imagine you can have one of the three works of art on this page. Which one are you going to choose? Why?

16 Please leave us a message.

1 CONVERSATION

🔊 Listen and practice.

Answering
  machine: Hi. This is Jennifer, and this is Nicole.
          We can't come to the phone right now.
          Please leave us a message, and . . . .
  Nicole: Hello?
  Michael: Hi. Nicole? It's Michael. Is Jennifer there?
  Nicole: Oh, hi, Michael. She's here, but she's in
          bed – she's sleeping. Can she call you later?
  Michael: Yeah, thanks. Please ask her to
           call me at my parents' house.
  Nicole: Sure. Just give me the number.
  Michael: It's 555-0367.
  Nicole: 555-0367. OK.
  Michael: Thanks a lot, Nicole.

2 WORD POWER Places

A 🔊 Listen and practice.

Jennifer can't come to the phone right now. . . .

She's **in** the shower.
       in the yard.
       in bed.

Jennifer isn't here right now. . . .

She's **at** the beach.   She's **in** the hospital.
      at her parents' house.   **in** South America.
      at the library.   **in** class.
      at the mall.
      at school.   She's **on** vacation.
      at home.   **on** a trip.
      at work.

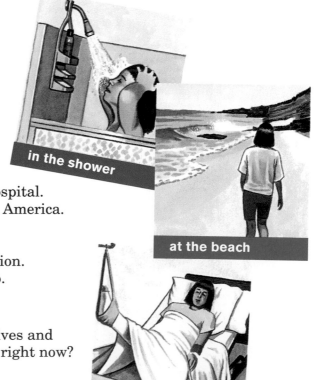

in the shower

at the beach

in the hospital

B *Pair work* Make a list of friends and relatives and
give it to your partner. Where are these people right now?
Ask and answer questions.

A: Where's your brother right now?
B: He's on a trip. He's in Thailand.

3 LISTENING

A  Listen to people making phone calls. Who are they calling? Write the names under the photos.

....
Jeff

B *Pair work* Take turns calling the people in part A.

A: Hello?
B: Hello. Is Jeff there, please?
A: I'm sorry, he can't come to the phone right now. He's in the shower.
B: OK. Thanks.

4 GRAMMAR FOCUS

Object pronouns

		Subject pronouns	Object pronouns	Subject pronouns	Object pronouns
Just give **me** the number.	Can I give **him** a message?	I →	me	it →	it
I don't have **it**.	Please leave **us** a message.	you →	you	we →	us
Can she call **you** later?	Please call **them** at work.	he →	him	you →	you
Give **her** a call later.	Please ask **her** to call **me**.	she →	her	they →	them

Complete these phone conversations. Then practice with a partner.

1. A: Is Sandra there, please?
   B: I'm sorry, she isn't here right now. Can I give ...*her*.... a message?
   A: Yes, this is David. Please ask .... to call .... at work.
   B: OK. Can you give .... your phone number, please?
   A: Sure. It's 555-2981.

2. A: Can I speak with Mr. Ford, please?
   B: He isn't here today. But maybe I can help ....
   A: Thanks. Can you ask .... to call .... ? This is John Rivers.
   B: John Rivers. Does he have your number, Mr. Rivers?
   A: Yes, he has ....

3. A: Hi. This is Carol and Mark. We can't come to the phone.
      Please leave .... a message after the beep. *Beep.*
   B: Hi. It's Betsy and James. Carol, you left your sunglasses here.
      We can bring .... to .... tomorrow. Just give .... a call.

5 *SNAPSHOT*

Ideas for a **FIRST DATE**

go to a concert or a play

go to an art gallery or a museum

see a movie

go dancing

visit a new place

go bike riding or hiking

have a picnic

Are these dating activities popular in your country?
What other activities are popular?
What are your favorite dating activities?

6 *CONVERSATION*

 Listen and practice.

Michael: Hello?
Jennifer: Hi, Michael. It's Jennifer. I got your
message.
Michael: Hi. Thanks for calling me back.
Jennifer: So, what's up?
Michael: Uh, well, do you want to have
dinner with me tomorrow night?
Jennifer: Tomorrow night? I'm really sorry, but
I can't. I have to stay home and study.
Michael: Oh, that's too bad. How about
Friday night?
Jennifer: Uh . . . sure. I'd love to. What time
do you want to meet?
Michael: How about around seven o'clock?
Jennifer: Terrific!

7 PRONUNCIATION Want to *and* have to

🔊 Listen and practice. Notice the pronunciation of
want to and **have to**.

/wanə/	/hæftə/
want to	**have to**

A: Do you **want to** see a movie with me tomorrow night?
B: I'm sorry, I can't. I **have to** stay home and study.
A: Do you **want to** go out on Friday night?
B: Sure. I really **want to** see the new James Bond movie.

see a movie

8 GRAMMAR FOCUS

Verb + to + verb; would 🔊

Accepting an invitation

Do you **want to see** a movie with me tomorrow?
   Yes, I**'d love to** (**see** a movie with you tomorrow).

I'd = I would

Refusing an invitation and making an excuse

Do you **want to have** dinner with me on Friday night?
   I'm sorry, but I can't. I **have to study**.
   Sorry, I **need to stay** home with my brother.
   Gee, I**'d like to**, but I **want to go** to bed early.

A Complete these responses with **'d love to**, **'d like to**,
have to, or **need to**. (More than one answer is sometimes
possible.)

Invitations

1. Do you want to go to the basketball
   game tomorrow night? ...c...

2. Do you want to see a movie
   with me tonight? ....

3. Do you want to go to the beach
   on Saturday? ....

4. Do you want to play volleyball
   after school today? ....

Responses

a. Tonight? I'm sorry, I can't.
   My parents are going to go out,
   and I .... baby-sit for my sister.

b. Sorry, I .... talk to the teacher
   after school.

c. Gee, I .... see the game, but
   I .... study for the exam
   on Thursday.

d. I .... go to the beach, but
   I can't. I .... go to the dentist
   on Saturday.

B Match the invitations with the responses in part A.
Then practice with a partner.

9 EXCUSES

A Do you use these excuses? Check (✓) **often**, **sometimes**, or **never**.
What are your three favorite excuses? Compare with a partner.

	Often	Sometimes	Never
I have to baby-sit.	☐	☐	☐
I need to study.	☐	☐	☐
I have to work late.	☐	☐	☐
I want to go to bed early.	☐	☐	☐
I want to visit my family.	☐	☐	☐
I have to go to class.	☐	☐	☐
I have a terrible headache.	☐	☐	☐
My back hurts.	☐	☐	☐
I need to stay home and clean.	☐	☐	☐
I have other plans.	☐	☐	☐

I have to baby-sit.

B Write down three things you want to do this weekend,
with the day and time.

I want to go to the ball game on Saturday night.

C *Class activity* Use your ideas from part B. Invite your classmates
to go with you.

A: Do you want to . . . on . . . ?
B: I'm sorry, but I can't. I have to . . . .
A: Do you want to . . . on . . . ?
C: I'd love to. What time do you want to meet?

10 LISTENING

A 🔊 Jennifer and Nicole invited some friends to a party on Saturday.
Listen to the messages on their answering machine. Who can come?
Who can't come? Check (✓) the correct answers.

	Can come	Can't come	Excuse
Steven	✓	☐	. . . .
Anna	☐	☐	. . . .
David	☐	☐	. . . .
Sarah	☐	☐	. . . .
Michael	☐	☐	. . . .

B 🔊 Listen again. For the friends who can't come, what excuse do they give?

11 *READING*

Free Activities This Weekend

What are some free activities in your city?

Craft Fair in Front of City Hall
Sunday from 9:00 A.M. to 5:00 P.M.

Need to buy a present? Find pottery, jewelry, paintings, sculpture, and more! Food from around the world, too!

Rock Concert at University Park
Saturday from 9:00 P.M. to midnight

Come hear some great music. Five terrific student bands are going to play. Bring your own food and drink.

City Museum Travel Movies
Saturday and Sunday at 2:30 P.M.

Do you want to travel, but don't have enough money? See movies on Japan, Indonesia, Brazil, Italy, and Australia. There are only 100 seats, so come early.

Library Lecture
City Library Auditorium Saturday at 10:00 A.M.

How to find the job you really want! Two-hour lecture. Advice on choosing and getting the right job for you. Sandwiches and soda sold.

Fall Fashion Show
Golden Shopping Plaza Sunday at 3:00 P.M.

Men's and women's fall clothes. See 25 fabulous models wearing the latest fashions. All clothing on sale after the show for under $100.

A Read the article. Then write two places where you can . . . .

1. buy clothes or jewelry ....
2. buy food ....
3. sit indoors ....
4. be outdoors ....

B *Pair work* List three things you want to do. Then compare with a partner. Is there one activity you both want to do?

First choice ....
Second choice ....
Third choice ....

interchange 16

Let's make a date!
Check your calendar and make a date. Student A turns to page IC-19. Student B turns to page IC-21.

Review of Units 13-16

1 NO, HE WASN'T!

Class activity Write three false statements about famous people using the simple past. Read your sentences to the class. Can anyone correct them?

> *Albert Einstein was a famous*
> *football player.*
> *Marilyn Monroe . . . .*

A: Albert Einstein was a famous football player.
B: No, he wasn't. He was a scientist.

2 LOCATIONS

A *Pair work* Take turns saying the location of these places. Say the location in two different ways.

1. parking lot
2. drugstore
3. dance club
4. bus stop
5. Japanese restaurant

A: The parking lot is on Second Avenue.
B: The parking lot is across from the Korean restaurant.

B *Pair work* Give directions to two places on the map. Your partner guesses the place.

A: Walk up First Avenue and turn left. It's on the right, on the corner of First and Lincoln.
B: It's the Japanese restaurant.
A: Right.

3 LISTENING

  Listen and check (✓) the correct response.

1. ☑ No, they weren't.
   ☐ No, they aren't.

2. ☐ At eleven o'clock.
   ☐ No, I didn't.

3. ☐ We took the bus.
   ☐ Amy and Katherine.

4. ☐ It was great.
   ☐ Sue and Tom were.

5. ☐ I'm going to visit my parents on Sunday.
   ☐ I had a terrible headache.

6. ☐ I'm sorry, but I can't go.
   ☐ No, I didn't go. I was at work.

7. ☐ I'm sorry, he's not here right now.
   ☐ Sandra is at work right now.

8. ☐ There's a restaurant on Grant Street.
   ☐ No, there isn't. Sorry.

4 CLASSROOM RULES

Write down four things you **have to** do in class.
Write down four things you **can't** do in class.
Compare with a partner.

You have to listen to the teacher.
You can't eat. . . .

5 TELL US ABOUT IT

A Group work Tell your classmates some of the things you did last week.
Each student then asks one question about it.

Tell them about . . . .
something you did last week that you liked
something you did last week that you didn't like
someone interesting you talked to last week
something interesting you bought last week

A: I saw a movie last week.
B: What was the name of the movie?
A: . . .
C: Who was in it?
A: . . .
D: How did you like it?
A: . . .

B Group work Make a list of four
things you want to do next week.
Tell the group about them.

I want to see the new James Bond movie.

Interchange Activities

DIRECTORY ASSISTANCE

Student A

A *Pair work* You are the customer. Student B is a telephone operator. Ask for the telephone numbers of these people.

Phone numbers	
Ms. Kumiko Sato	....
Ms. Ana Sanchez	....
Mr. Mark Saunders	....
Mr. Anan Songsawat	....

Operator: Directory Assistance.
Customer: Hello. What's the number for . . . ?
Operator: How do you spell the last name?
Customer: . . .
Operator: And the first name?
Customer: . . .
Operator: Thank you. The number is . . . .

B *Pair work* Change roles. You are a telephone operator. Student B asks for some telephone numbers. Find the numbers in the directory.

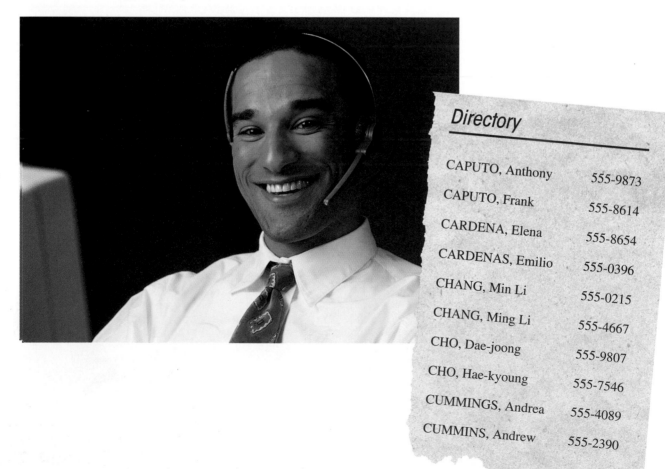

Directory

CAPUTO, Anthony	555-9873
CAPUTO, Frank	555-8614
CARDENA, Elena	555-8654
CARDENAS, Emilio	555-0396
CHANG, Min Li	555-0215
CHANG, Ming Li	555-4667
CHO, Dae-joong	555-9807
CHO, Hae-kyoung	555-7546
CUMMINGS, Andrea	555-4089
CUMMINS, Andrew	555-2390

interchange 2 FIND THE DIFFERENCES

A *Pair work* How are the two pictures different?
Ask questions to find the differences.

A: Where are the sunglasses?
B: In picture 1, they're on the television.
A: In picture 2, they're behind the television.

Picture 1

Picture 2

B *Class activity* Talk about the differences with your classmates.

"In picture 1, the sunglasses are on the television. In picture 2, they're behind the television."

interchange 1 *DIRECTORY ASSISTANCE*

Student B

A *Pair work* You are a telephone operator. Student A is the customer. Student A asks for some telephone numbers. Find the numbers in the directory.

Directory	
SANCHES, Ada	555-2576
SANCHEZ, Ana	555-3519
SANDERS, Carl	555-8125
SATO, Hiroshi	555-9012
SATO, Kumiko	555-6734
SAUNDERS, Mark	555-1329
SILVA, Roberto	555-3418
SILVER, Roberta	555-0926
SONGSAWAT, Amara	555-6775
SONGSAWAT, Anan	555-2258

Operator: Directory Assistance.
Customer: Hello. What's the number for . . . ?
Operator: How do you spell the last name?
Customer: . . .
Operator: And the first name?
Customer: . . .
Operator: Thank you. The number is . . . .

B *Pair work* Change roles. You are the customer, and Student A is a telephone operator. Ask for the numbers of these people.

Phone numbers	
Ms. Min Li Chang	. . . .
Mr. Frank Caputo	. . . .
Miss Andrea Cummings	. . . .
Mr. Dae-joong Cho	. . . .

interchange **3** **CLASS PERSONALITIES**

A Read the chart and add two more descriptions. Look around your class and complete the chart. Write names of classmates.

Who's . . . ?	Name
really friendly	....
tall and good-looking	....
very smart	....
talkative	....
serious and a little shy	....
unusual and interesting	....
really funny	....
....	....
....	....

talkative

unusual

B *Group work* Compare your answers in part A.

A: Who's really friendly?
B: Sun-hee is really friendly.
C: Yes, and Yong-joon is friendly, too.

interchange 4 CELEBRITY FASHIONS

Group work Take turns. Describe the people at the party.
Don't say the person's name. Your classmates guess who it is.

A: He's wearing blue jeans, a yellow shirt,
   and a black jacket. Who is it?
B: Is it Leonardo DiCaprio?
A: No, it isn't.
C: Is it Will Smith?
A: That's right.

A: They're both wearing dresses. Who are they?
B: Are they Susan Sarandon and Kate Winslet?
A: That's right.

Jennifer Lopez

Denzel Washington

Antonio Banderas

Cameron Diaz

Leonardo DiCaprio

Chayanne

Susan Sarandon

Jackie Chan

Tom Cruise

interchange 5 *TIME ZONES*

Pair work Ask and answer questions about the cities on the map.
Use expressions from the box.

sleeping	shopping
getting up	going home
having breakfast	cooking
going to work	having dinner
working	watching television
having lunch	going to bed

A: What time is it in Los Angeles?
B: It's 4:00 A.M./It's four o'clock in the morning.
A: What are people doing there?
B: They're sleeping.

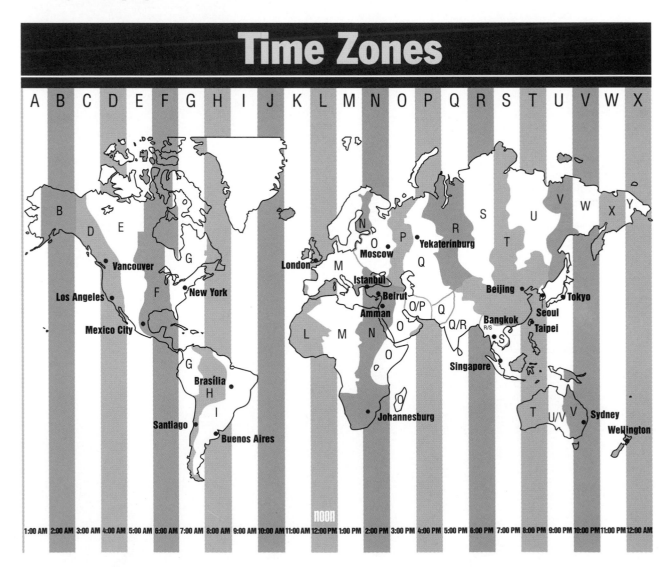

interchange 6 CLASS SURVEY

A *Class activity* Go around the class and find this information.
If possible, write a classmate's name only once.

Find someone who			
	Name		**Name**
gets up at 5:00 A.M. on weekdays	....	rides a bicycle to class	....
gets up at noon on Saturdays	....	rides a motorcycle to class	....
has breakfast in bed	....	walks to class	....
works at night	....	goes on the Internet every day	....
works on weekends	....	doesn't own a computer	....
lives downtown	....	wears blue jeans every day	....
lives in the country	....	speaks three languages	....
lives alone	....		

having breakfast in bed

riding a motorcycle to class

Hello?
Allô?
Moshi Moshi!

speaking three languages

A: Do you get up at 5:00 A.M.?
B: No, I get up at 7:00 A.M.
A: Do you get up at 5:00 A.M.?
C: Yes, I get up at 5:00 A.M. every day.

B *Group work* Compare your information.

A: Keiko gets up at 5:00 A.M.
B: Akira gets up at 5:00 A.M., too.

interchange 7 *FIND THE DIFFERENCES*

Bill's apartment

Jane's apartment

A Write five differences between Bill's apartment and Jane's apartment.

There are four chairs in Bill's kitchen. There are only three chairs in Jane's kitchen.
There's a sofa in Bill's living room, but there's no sofa in Jane's living room.

....

....

....

....

....

B *Pair work* Compare your answers.

interchange 8 THE PERFECT JOB

A *Pair work* You're looking for a job. Which of these things do you want in a job? First, answer the questions. Then ask your partner the same questions.

Job Survey	Me		My Partner	
Do you want to . . . ?	Yes	No	Yes	No
talk to people	☐	☐	☐	☐
help people	☐	☐	☐	☐
perform in front of people	☐	☐	☐	☐
work from 9 to 5	☐	☐	☐	☐
work at home	☐	☐	☐	☐
use a computer	☐	☐	☐	☐
use the telephone	☐	☐	☐	☐
work in an office	☐	☐	☐	☐
have your own office	☐	☐	☐	☐
work outdoors	☐	☐	☐	☐
travel	☐	☐	☐	☐
have an exciting job	☐	☐	☐	☐
have a relaxing job	☐	☐	☐	☐
wear a uniform	☐	☐	☐	☐
wear a suit	☐	☐	☐	☐
wear blue jeans	☐	☐	☐	☐

work from 9 to 5

work outdoors

B *Class activity* Think of a good job for yourself. Then tell the class.

"I want to be a musician because I want to work at home. . . ."

work at home   perform in front of people   travel

interchange 9 *EATING HABITS*

A Complete this survey about the foods you eat.
Use these foods and other foods you know.

chicken · onions · popcorn · green beans · peppers · tuna · peaches · garlic · chocolates · pineapple · grapes · hot dogs · watermelon · shrimp · steak

Things I eat	every day	two/three times a week	about once a week
meat/fish			
dairy			
fruits			
vegetables			
snacks			
other foods			

B *Pair work* Compare your information.

A: I eat chicken once a week.
B: I never eat chicken. I eat steak once a week. . . .

C *Class activity* What are the class's favorite foods?

interchange **10** *HIDDEN TALENTS*

A *Class activity* Go around the class and find one person who *can* and one person who *can't* do each thing. If possible, write a classmate's name only once.

Names		
Can you . . . ?	**Can**	**Can't**
play a musical instrument	....	....
dance the tango	....	....
say "Hello" in 5 languages	....	....
swim underwater	....	....
write with both hands	....	....
sing a song in English	....	....
ride a horse	....	....
juggle	....	....
sew your own clothes	....	....
do magic tricks	....	....

dance the tango   write with both hands   ride a horse

juggle   sew your own clothes   do magic tricks

A: Can you play a musical instrument?
B: Yes, I can. **OR** No, I can't.

B *Class activity* Share your results with the class.

"Mei-Li can't play a musical instrument, but Wen Pin can."

interchange 11 CELEBRATIONS

A *Pair work* What are these people doing? What are they going to do?
Write a story for each picture. Use these expressions and your own ideas.

have a party	receive a diploma
shout "Happy New Year!"	get some presents
see friends	wear special hats
listen to a speech	have a good time
sing "Happy Birthday"	have a picnic
blow out the candles	barbecue hamburgers
open the presents	watch the fireworks

2. It's Jessica's high school graduation. . . .

1. It's New Year's Eve. . . .

> *They're having a party.*
> *They're going to shout*
> *"Happy New Year!" . . .*

4. It's the Fourth of July in the U.S. . . .

3. It's Jeremy's birthday. . . .

B *Group work* Join another pair. Compare your stories.

interchange 12 *HELPFUL ADVICE*

A *Pair work* Look at these problems. Give advice to each person.

I can't lose weight. I really like dessert. Cake is my favorite food!

My job is very stressful. I usually work 10 hours a day and on weekends. I have backaches and headaches almost every day.

I can never get up on time in the morning. I'm always late for work. I guess I'm not a morning person.

I'm new in town, and I don't know any people here. How can I make some friends?

B *Class activity* Think of two problems that you have. Then tell the class. Classmates give advice.

A: I can't sleep at night.
B: Get up and do some work.
C: Don't drink coffee in the evening.

interchange 13 *DIRECTIONS*

Student A

A *Pair work* Look at the map. You are on Third Avenue between Maple and Oak Streets. Ask your partner for directions to the places below. (On your map there are no signs on these places.) Write the name of each place on the correct building.

a car wash   a supermarket   a flower shop

A: Excuse me. Is there a car wash near here?   A: How do I get there?
B: Yes, there's a car wash . . . .   B: . . .

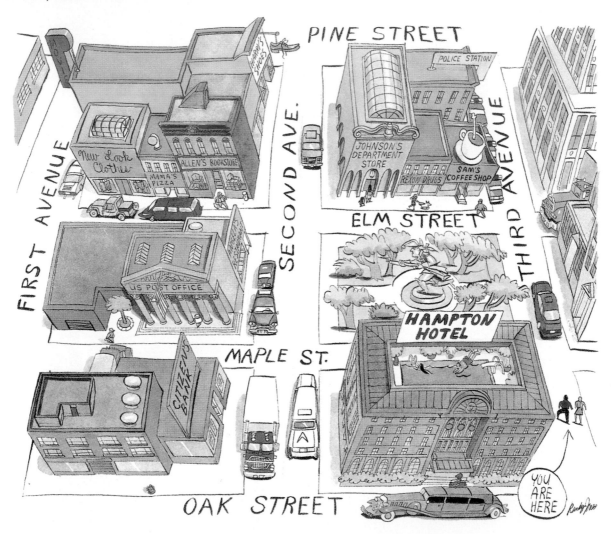

B *Pair work* Your partner asks you for directions to three places. (There are signs for these places only on your map.) Give your partner directions. Use the expressions in the box.

Go up/Go down	It's on the corner of . . . Street	It's next to . . . .
Walk one block	and . . . Avenue.	It's behind . . . .
Turn right/Turn left	It's between . . . and	It's in front of . . . .
	It's across from	

interchange 14 *PAST AND PRESENT*

A *Pair work* Ask a partner questions about the past
and about the present. Check (✓) the answers.

A: Did you clean your room as a child?
B: No, I didn't. (Yes, I did.)

A: Do you clean your room now?
B: Yes, I do. (No, I don't.)

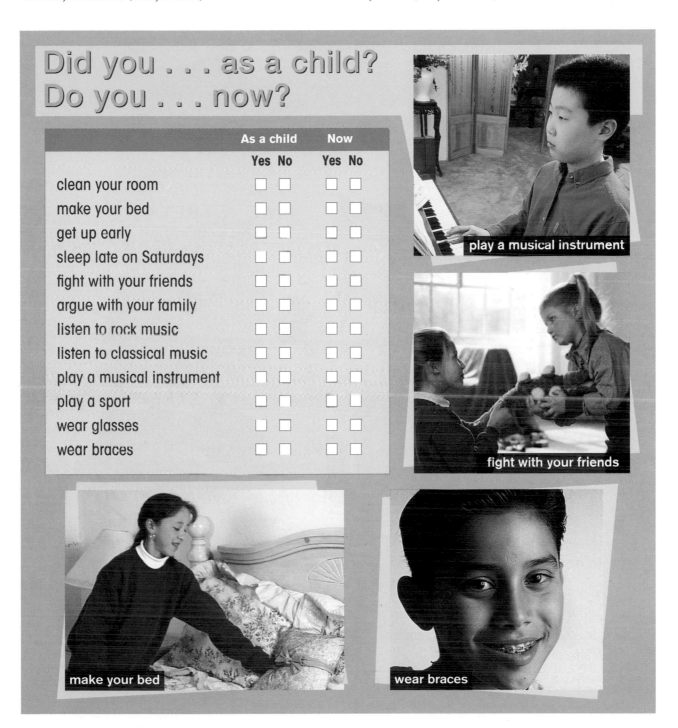

Did you . . . as a child?
Do you . . . now?

	As a child		Now	
	Yes	No	Yes	No
clean your room	☐	☐	☐	☐
make your bed	☐	☐	☐	☐
get up early	☐	☐	☐	☐
sleep late on Saturdays	☐	☐	☐	☐
fight with your friends	☐	☐	☐	☐
argue with your family	☐	☐	☐	☐
listen to rock music	☐	☐	☐	☐
listen to classical music	☐	☐	☐	☐
play a musical instrument	☐	☐	☐	☐
play a sport	☐	☐	☐	☐
wear glasses	☐	☐	☐	☐
wear braces	☐	☐	☐	☐

play a musical instrument

fight with your friends

make your bed

wear braces

B *Group work* Join another pair. Tell them about your partner.

"Paulo didn't clean his room as a child, but he cleans his room now."

interchange 13 DIRECTIONS

Student B

A *Pair work* Look at the map. You are on Third Avenue between Maple and Oak Streets. Your partner asks you for directions to three places. (There are signs for these places only on your map.) Answer using the expressions in the box.

A: Excuse me. Is there a car wash near here?   A: How do I get there?
B: Yes, there's a car wash . . . .   B: . . .

Go up/Go down	It's on the corner of . . . Street	It's next to . . . .
Walk one block	and . . . Avenue.	It's behind . . . .
Turn right/Turn left	It's between . . . and	It's in front of . . . .
	It's across from	

B *Pair work* Ask your partner for directions to the places below. (On your map there are no signs on these places.) Write the name of each place on the correct building.

coffee shop   shoe store   bookstore

interchange 16 | ***LET'S MAKE A DATE!***

Student A

A *Pair work* This is your calendar for March. You want to make an evening date with your partner. Ask and answer questions to find a date.

A: Do you want to go out on March third?
B: I'd like to, but I can't. I'm going to go ice-skating with Mary. How about . . . ?

MARCH

SUNDAY	MONDAY	TUESDAY	WEDNESDAY	THURSDAY	FRIDAY	SATURDAY
1 visit my parents	2 go to my tennis class	3	4 go to the dentist	5	6 have dinner with Ken	7
8	9 go to my tennis class	10	11 go dancing	12	13	14 go to Bill's birthday party
15	16	17	18	19	20	21
		v a c a t i o n !				
22	23 go to my tennis class	24	25 meet David, Linda, and Amy	26	27	28
29 go out with David's friend	30	31 go to the movies with Jane				

B *Pair work* Now you have a date. Discuss the possibilities. Decide what to do.

A: Do you want to play tennis?
B: No, I don't play tennis very well.
   Do you want to go to a museum?
A: No, I don't like museums. . . .

C *Class activity* Tell the class your plan.

interchange 15 *TIME LINE*

A What are five important events in your life? Mark the dates on the time line. Then write a sentence about each one.

I was born . . . .

I graduated from high school . . . .

I got my first job . . . .

I started college . . . .

I moved into my first apartment/house . . . .

I fell in love . . . .

I got married . . . .

My first child was born . . . .

1960   1970   1980   1990   2000

I was born in 1974.

1. ....
2. ....
3. ....
4. ....
5. ....

B *Pair work* Find out your partner's five important years.
Then take turns. Ask and answer questions about the important years.

A: What happened in 1997?
B: I fell in love.
A: How old were you?
B: I was twenty-three.
A: . . .

interchange 16 *LET'S MAKE A DATE!*

Student B

A *Pair work* This is your calendar for March. You want to make an evening date with your partner. Ask and answer questions to find a date.

A: Do you want to go out on March third?
B: I'd like to, but I can't. I'm going to go ice-skating with Mary. How about . . . ?

MARCH

Sunday	Monday	Tuesday	Wednesday	Thursday	Friday	Saturday
1	2	3 *go ice-skating with Mary*	4 *have dinner with Sue – Thai restaurant?*	5 *go to my guitar lesson*	6 *see a movie with Joe*	7
8 *visit my parents*	9	10 *go swimming with Jenny*	11	12 *go to my guitar lesson*	13 *go to the Madonna concert*	14
15	16 *go to Frank's party*	17 *have dinner with Ken*	18	19 *go to my guitar lesson*	20	21
22	23 *V A C A*	24 *T I*	25 *O N*	26 *go to my guitar lesson*	27	28 *visit my grand-parents*
29	30 *go shopping with my parents*	31				

B *Pair work* Now you have a date. Discuss the possibilities. Decide what to do.

A: Do you want to play tennis?
B: No, I don't play tennis very well.
   Do you want to go to a museum?
A: No, I don't like museums. . . .

C *Class activity* Tell the class your plan.

Unit Summaries

Unit Summaries contain lists of key vocabulary and functional expressions. Key vocabulary is listed in the unit in which a word first appears. For Grammar Focus models, please refer to the appropriate unit page.

1 IT'S NICE TO MEET YOU.

KEY VOCABULARY

Nouns
The alphabet
See Exercise 4 on page 3.

Numbers (1–10)
See Exercise 10 on page 6.

Titles
Miss
Mr.
Mrs.
Ms.

Parts of the day
morning
afternoon
evening
night

Other
book
(English/math) class
classmate
country
female
male
(first/last) name
(tele)phone number
teacher

Pronouns
Subject pronouns
I
you
he
she
it

Adjectives
Possessives
my
your
his
her

Other
favorite
first
last
popular

Verbs
am ('m)
are ('re)
is ('s)

Adverbs
Responses
no
yes

Other
again
(over) there
too

Preposition
in (my class)

Conjunction
and

Interjection
oh

EXPRESSIONS

Saying hello
Good morning/afternoon/evening.
Hello./Hi.
How are you?
   (I'm) great. Thank you./Thanks.
      (just) fine.
      not bad.
      OK.

Saying good-bye
Good-bye./Bye./Bye-bye.
Good night.
See you later/tomorrow.
Have a good evening/a nice day.
   Thanks./You, too.

Introducing yourself
Hi. My name is . . . .
   I'm . . . .
It's nice to meet you, ...
   Nice to meet you, too.

Exchanging personal information
What's your name?
   I'm . . . . / My name is . . . .
What's your phone number?
   It's . . . .

Checking and confirming information
What's your last name again?
   It's . . . .
How do you spell . . . ?
Is that . . . ?
   Yes, that's right./No, it's . . . .
Are you . . . ?
   No, I'm not./Yes, I am.

Introducing someone
. . . , this is . . . .
   Hi, ... It's nice to meet you.

Apologizing
I'm sorry.

Getting someone's attention
Excuse me.

Giving an opinion
I think . . . .

2 WHAT'S THIS?

KEY VOCABULARY

Nouns
Classroom objects
board
book
book bag
calculator
cassette player
chair
clock
desk
(English) dictionary
encyclopedia
eraser
map
notebook
pen
pencil
table
wastebasket

Personal items
address
(electronic) address book
bag
briefcase
camera
CD player
cell phone

earring(s)
glasses
(car) keys
newspaper
pager
purse
stamp
sunglasses
(tele)phone
television
umbrella
wallet
watch

Other
box
chopsticks
classroom
door
exercise
location
pocket
restaurant
sentence
thing
wall
window

Pronouns
Demonstratives
that
these
this

Subject pronoun
they

Adjectives
gone
great
interesting
nice

Articles
a/an
the

Verbs
bet
open
relax
spell

Adverbs
still
very

Prepositions
behind
in
in front of
next to
on
under

Interjections
hmm
No problem.
Oh, cool!
Oh, no!
OK.
See?
uh
Wait!
Wow!

EXPRESSIONS

Identifying objects
What's this called in English?
  I don't know.
  It's a/an . . . .
What are these called in English?
  They're . . . .

Finding the owner of an item
Is this your . . . ?
  Yes, it is./No, it's not. It's . . . .
Are these his . . . ?
  Yes, they are./No, they're not. They're . . . .

Asking for and giving location
Where is . . . ?
  It's under/. . . the . . . .
Where are . . . ?
  They're under/. . . the . . . .

Checking information
How do you spell that?

Making a request
Let me . . . .

Thanking someone
Thank you.
  You're welcome.

Realizing something
Wait a minute!

3 WHERE ARE YOU FROM?

KEY VOCABULARY

Nouns
*Countries, Nationalities,
and Languages*
See the appendix.

Regions of the world
Africa
Asia
Australia, New Zealand,
   and Pacific Islands
(the) Caribbean
Central America
Europe
North America
South America

People
best friend
brother
family
mother
parents
person (*plural* = people)
sister
student

Places
city (*plural* = cities)
world

Other
college
language

Pronouns
Subject pronouns
we
you (*plural*)

Adjectives
Describing people
cute
friendly
funny
good-looking
handsome
heavy
nice
pretty
serious
short
shy
smart
tall
thin

*Numbers and ages (11–30;
40, 50, etc.)*
See Exercise 6 on page 17.

Other
beautiful
fine
large
new
old

Verbs
call
know
think

Adverbs
a little
here
originally
really
so
this week
today

Prepositions
from (Seoul)
in (the United States)

EXPRESSIONS

**Asking about countries, nationalities,
and languages**
Are you from Seoul/. . . ?
   Yes, I am./No, I'm not. I'm from . . . .
Where is he/she from?
   He's/She's from . . . .
Are you Japanese/. . . ?
   Yes, we are./No, we're not. We're . . . .
Is your first language English/. . . ?
   Yes, it is./No, it's not.

Asking about people
Who are they?/Who's that?/What are their names?
   He's . . . , and she's . . . .
Where are they from?
   They're from . . . .
What are they like?
   They're very/really . . . .

ANSWER KEY   Unit 3, Exercise 6, page 17

Antonio Banderas: Born in 1960.
Yuka Honda: Doesn't tell her age.
What is your guess?

Nelson Mandela: Born in 1918.
Celine Dion: Born in 1968.

Pelé: Born in 1940.
Se Ri Pak: Born in 1977.

4 I'M NOT WEARING BOOTS!

KEY VOCABULARY

Nouns
Clothes
belt
blouse
boot(s)
cap
coat
dress
glove(s)
hat
(high) heels
jacket
jeans
pajamas
pants
raincoat
running shoes
scarf
shirt
shoe(s)
shorts
skirt
sneakers
sock(s)
suit
sweater
sweatshirt
swimsuit
T-shirt
tie

Seasons of the year
spring
summer
fall
winter

Other
clothes
matter
problem
season
taxi
weather

Adjectives
Colors
beige
black
(dark/light) blue
(dark/light) brown
(dark/light) gray
(dark/light) green
orange
pink
purple
red
white
yellow

Weather
cloudy
cold
cool
hot
humid
sunny
warm
windy

Possessives
our
your *(plural)*
their

Other
dry
important
ruined

Verbs
rain
snow
take (a taxi)
wear

Adverbs
actually
probably

Conjunction
but

Interjections
Uh-oh!
Yeah.

EXPRESSIONS

Talking about preferences
What's your favorite color?
  My favorite color is . . . .

Asking about and describing clothing
What color is/are . . . ?
  It's/They're . . . .
Are you wearing . . . ?
  Yes, I am./No, I'm not. I'm wearing . . . .

Showing opposition
I'm . . . , but I'm not . . . .

Talking about the weather
It's snowing/raining/. . . .
It's cloudy/cold/hot/sunny/. . . .

5 WHAT ARE YOU DOING?

KEY VOCABULARY

Nouns
Meals
breakfast
lunch
dinner

Form of address
Mom

Other
bike
conference
friend
hometown
movie
pizza
tennis
time zone
walk
work

Adjectives
awake
hungry
sorry

Verbs
cook
dance
do
drive
eat
get up
go (to work/to the movies)
have (breakfast/lunch/dinner)
make
play (tennis)
read
remember
ride (a bike)
run
shop
sleep
study
swim
take (a walk)
watch (television)
work

Adverbs
Times
at midnight/at noon
at night
in the afternoon
in the evening
in the morning

Clock times
A.M./P.M.
midnight
noon
o'clock

Other
(right) now

Prepositions
after (six)
at (six o'clock)
to (six)

Conjunction
so

Interjection
mmm

EXPRESSIONS

Asking for and telling time
What time is it?
  It's . . . o'clock (in the morning/. . .).
  It's . . . after . . . .
  It's a quarter after . . . .
  It's . . . -thirty.
  It's a quarter to . . . .

Asking about and describing current activities
What are you doing?
  I'm . . . .
Are you . . . ?
  Yes, I am./No, I'm not. I'm . . . .

Giving a reason
What's he doing?
  It's . . . , so he's . . . .

Making a suggestion
Let's . . . .

Checking information
 . . . . Right?
  Yes.

Responding to an apology
I'm really sorry.
  That's OK.

Talking on the telephone
Hello?
  Hi, ... This is . . . .

6 WE LIVE IN THE SUBURBS.

KEY VOCABULARY

Nouns

Hometown areas
country
downtown
suburbs

Modes of transportation
bus
bus station
car
ferry
ferry terminal
public transportation
subway
subway station
taxi
taxi stand
train
train station

Hometown places
apartment
house
office
park
restaurant
school
store

Family relationships
brother
children/kids
daughter
father/dad
husband
mother/mom
parents
sister
son
wife

Days of the week
Monday
Tuesday
Wednesday
Thursday
Friday
Saturday
Sunday

Other
computer
day
homework
Internet
paper
(flat) tire
weekday
weekend

Pronouns
Object pronouns
me
us

Determiners
all (day)
both
every (day)

Adjectives
busy
good
lucky
public
retired

Verbs
come
do (work)
go (to school/to bed)
go on (the Internet)
live
meet
need
say
serve
take (a bus/a train)
use
wait (for)
walk

Adverbs
Times
early
every day
late

Other
a lot of
alone
also
far
home
then
together
yet

Prepositions
at (home)
by (bus/car)
for (people like us)
like (us)
near (here)
on (Sundays/weekends)
with (my parents)

EXPRESSIONS

Talking about routines
What time do you . . . ?
  At . . . .
When does he . . . ?
  He . . . at . . . .
Does he . . . ?
  Yes, he . . . every morning/. . . .
How do you go to . . . ?
  I . . . .

Expressing an opinion
That's good.
You're lucky!

Expressing agreement
Yeah.
Sure.

Saying hello
Hey.

7 DOES THE APARTMENT HAVE A VIEW?

KEY VOCABULARY

Nouns
Houses and apartments
bathroom
bedroom
closet
dining room
elevator
(first/second) floor
garage
hall
kitchen
laundry room
living room
lobby
(swimming) pool
room
stairs
yard

Furniture
armchair
bed
bookcase
chair
clock

coffee table
curtain(s)
desk
dresser
lamp
mirror
picture
rug
sofa
table

Appliances
microwave oven
refrigerator
stove

Other
neighbor
river
view

Determiners
any
no
some

Adjectives
big
dream (house)
own (room)
super

Verbs
buy
go shopping
love

Prepositions
on (Lakeview Drive)
in (the country/the city)

EXPRESSIONS

Asking about and describing a home
What's the house/apartment like?
   It's beautiful/. . . . / It has . . . .
Does it have . . . ?
   Yes, it does./No, it doesn't.
Do you live/have . . . ?
   Yes, I do./No, I don't.

Talking about quantity
How many rooms/. . . does it have?
   It has . . . . / There's one . . . . / There are . . . .

Saying what there is and isn't
There's a/an . . . .
There isn't a/an . . . . / There's no . . . .
There are some . . . .
There aren't any . . . . / There are no . . . .

Asking for more information
What else does it have?

Telling someone surprising news
Guess what!

Responding to news
That's super.
That sounds nice.

Giving and responding to compliments
This . . . is great.
   Thanks.
   Oh, nice.

WHAT DO YOU DO?

KEY VOCABULARY

Nouns

Jobs/Occupations
accountant
actor
air traffic controller
artist
athlete
carpenter (carpentry)
cashier
cook/chef
DJ (disc jockey)
doctor
fashion designer
firefighter
flight attendant
florist
gardener
judge
lawyer
librarian
(rock) musician
nurse
photographer
pilot
police officer
receptionist
repairperson
salesperson
security guard
singer
waiter
waitress

Places
department store
electronics store
factory
hospital
hotel
office

Other
break
gun
money
opinion
relative
uniform
woman (*plural* = women)

Adjectives
boring
dangerous
difficult
easy
exciting
relaxing
safe
stressful
terrific

Verbs
agree
carry
disagree
finish
handle
hear
like
look for
repair
sell
sit
stand
start
take (a break)
talk (to)
teach

Adverbs
all day
exactly
hard

EXPRESSIONS

Exchanging information about work
Where do you work?
  I work in a/an . . . .
What do you do there?
  I'm a/an . . . .
When do you start/finish work?
  I start/finish work at . . . .
Do you take a break in the afternoon?
What do you do after work?
  I . . . .
Where does your brother work?
  He works . . . .
What does he do, exactly?
  He's a/an . . . .

Asking for and giving opinions about jobs
How do you like it?
  It's . . . .
A/An . . . has a/an boring/ . . . job.
  I agree. A/An . . .'s job is very . . . .
  I disagree. A/An . . . doesn't have a/an . . . job. It's . . . .

Exchanging personal information
How are things with you?
  Not bad.

Expressing sympathy
That's too bad.

Expressing surprise
Really?

Giving more information
. . . , you know.

9 BROCCOLI IS GOOD FOR YOU.

KEY VOCABULARY

Nouns

Dairy foods
cheese
milk
yogurt

Desserts
cake
cookie(s)
ice cream
pie

Fat, Oil, Sugar
butter
candy
cream
oil
potato chips

Fruit
apple(s)
banana(s)
grape(s)
mango(es)
orange(s)
strawberry (-ies)
tangerine(s)

Meat / Protein
bacon
bean(s)
beef
chicken
egg(s)
fish
hamburger(s)
nut(s)

Grains
bread
cereal
cracker(s)
noodles
pasta
rice
rolls
toast

Salads
fruit salad
potato salad

Vegetables
broccoli
carrot(s)
celery
lettuce
onion(s)
potato(es)
tomato(es)

Beverages
lemonade
soda
(green) tea

Other
barbecue
freezer
grocery store
health
mayonnaise
snacks
soup

Pronouns
everyone
something

Determiners
any
some

Adjectives
awful
delicious
(Japanese)-style

Verbs
drink
get
hate
try
want

Adverbs
Adverbs of frequency
always
ever
never
often
seldom
sometimes
usually

Prepositions
at (my desk)
for (breakfast/the barbecue)
in (the salad)

EXPRESSIONS

Talking about likes and dislikes
I love oranges.
Everyone likes potato salad.
I hate onions.
I think . . . is/are delicious/awful.
. . . is/are my favorite . . . .

Talking about things you need
Do you need any . . . ?
　Yes, we need some . . . .
　No, we don't need any . . . .
What do you need?

Asking about eating habits
What time do you eat breakfast/lunch/dinner?
What do you usually have for breakfast/lunch/dinner?
Do you ever eat . . . for breakfast/lunch/dinner?
Do you ever go to a restaurant for breakfast/lunch/dinner?
Do you always drink the same thing
　in the morning/afternoon/evening?
What is something you never have for
　breakfast/lunch/dinner?

Determining what is healthy
For good health, eat a lot of . . . /
　eat some . . . /eat very little . . . .
. . . is/are very good for you.

Giving an opinion
I think . . . .

Making a suggestion
How about . . . ?

Hesitating
Hmm.

Expressing agreement
All right.
Good idea.
Oh, yeah.
OK.

KEY VOCABULARY

Nouns
Sports
baseball
basketball
bike riding
football
golf
hiking
hockey
ice-skating
skiing
soccer
swimming
tennis
volleyball

Other
ability
beach
guitar
piano
poetry
talent
talent show
team
(free) time

Adjectives
artistic
athletic
great
mechanical
musical
technical

Verbs
draw
enjoy
enter
fix
play (a musical instrument)
play (a sport)
practice
sing
skate
speak
use (computers)
write

Adverbs
(not) at all
just
maybe
tomorrow
too
(not) very well
(really) well

Preposition
on (TV)

EXPRESSIONS

Talking about sports
What sports do you like/play . . . ?
  I love/play . . . .
  I don't like/play . . . .
  I like . . . , but I really love . . . .
Who do you play . . . with?
  With some friends from work.
When does your team practice?
  We practice on . . . .
What time do you practice?
  We start at . . . .
Where do you go skiing?
  I go skiing in Colorado.

Asking for and giving an opinion
What do you think of . . . ?
  I think it's dangerous/. . . .

Talking about abilities and talents
Can you . . . ?
  Yes, I can./No, I can't.
Can they . . . ?
  Yes, they can . . . very well.
  No, they can't . . . at all.
I can . . . , but I can't . . . very well.

Agreeing to do something
Sure. Why not?

Complimenting someone
You're a really good . . . !
You can . . . really well.
  Thanks.

11 WHAT ARE YOU GOING TO DO?

KEY VOCABULARY

Nouns
Months of the year
January
February
March
April
May
June
July
August
September
October
November
December

Other
birthday
gym
mashed potatoes
parade
party
picnic
plans
present
turkey

Pronoun
anything

Adjectives
Ordinal numbers (1–31)
See Exercise 1 on page 66.

Other
different
embarrassing
holiday
next
same
special
unusual

Verbs
ask (= invite)
celebrate
end
go out
have (a party/a picnic)
invite
order
see (a movie)
stay (home)
take (someone to a restaurant)
think about

Adverbs
around (midnight)
tonight

Preposition
for (Thanksgiving/your birthday)

EXPRESSIONS

Talking about future plans
Are you going to do anything exciting this/next . . . ?
    Yes, I am. I'm going to . . . .
    No, I'm not. I'm going to . . . .
What are your plans?/Any plans?
    I'm going to . . . .
What are you going to do?
    I'm going to . . . .
Where are you going to go?
    I'm going to go to . . . .
Who's going to be there?
    . . . is/are going to be there.
When are you going to go?
    We're going to . . . .
How are you going to get there?
    We're going to . . . .

Talking about dates
When is your birthday?
    It's August ninth.

Talking about holidays
What are you going to do for Thanksgiving?
    I'm going to have dinner at my parents' house.

Greeting someone on a special day
Happy birthday!
    Thanks.
Have a happy Thanksgiving/. . . .
    Thanks. You, too.

Asking for more information
What about you?

Expressing an opinion
Hmm. That's unusual.
(That) sounds like fun.

Giving a positive reaction
Fabulous!
Nice!

KEY VOCABULARY

Nouns
Parts of the body
ankle
arm
back
chest
chin
ear
elbow
eye
finger(s)
foot (*plural* = feet)
hand
head
knee
leg
mouth
neck
nose
shoulder
stomach
throat
thumb
toe(s)
tooth (*plural* = teeth)
wrist

Health problems
backache
cold
cough
earache
fever
the flu
headache
sore (eyes/throat)
stomachache
toothache

Medications
antacid
aspirin
cold pills
cough drops
cough syrup
eyedrops
muscle cream

Other
bath
coffee
fun
idea
juice
look
patient

Adjectives
Feelings
awful
bad
exhausted
fine (well)
good (better)
great
happy
homesick
sad
sick
terrible
terrific
tired

Other
sore
wrong

Verbs
feel
guess
help
hope
lift
lose (weight)
miss
point
stay (in bed)
stay up (late)
take (a bath)
take (a look at)
take (medicine)

Adverbs
already
soon
too

Prepositions
for (ten minutes)
in (bed/the house)
on (the phone)

EXPRESSIONS

Talking about health problems
How are you?
  I'm not so good, actually.
What's the matter?/What's wrong?
  I have . . . .
How do you feel?
  I feel sick/. . . .
  I don't feel well.
  I feel better already.

Expressing sympathy
That's too bad.
I'm sorry to hear that.
I hope you feel better soon.

Giving instructions/advice
Take/Don't take . . . .
Go to/Don't go to . . . .
Eat/Don't eat . . . .
Do/Don't do . . . .

13 YOU CAN'T MISS IT.

KEY VOCABULARY

Nouns
Places
bank
bookstore
bridge
cathedral
coffee shop
department store
drugstore
gas station
library
movie theater
museum
post office
restaurant
shoe store
statue
supermarket

Form of address
ma'am

Other
block
building
gasoline
rest room
sandwich
traveler's checks

Adjective
other

Verbs
get (to)
miss (something)
turn around

Adverbs
around
down
left
right
up

Prepositions
across from
behind
between
near
next to
on (Main Street)
on the corner of

EXPRESSIONS

Asking for and giving locations
Is there a/an . . . around here?
    Yes, there is. It's next to/across from/. . . .
Where's the . . . ? Is it far from here?
    It's right behind you.

Asking for and giving directions
How do I get to . . . ?
    Walk up/Go up . . . (to . . .).
    Walk down/Go down . . . for . . . block(s).
    Turn right/Turn left at/on . . . .
    It's on the right./It's on the left.
    You can't miss it.

Saying where you can buy things
You can buy cough drops at a drugstore.

Asking for help
Excuse me, ma'am. Can you help me?

Checking information
The . . . is on the corner of . . . and . . . .
    On the corner of . . . and . . . ?

KEY VOCABULARY

Nouns
bill
chore
cup
dance club
girlfriend
groceries
laundry
letter
mall
meal
popcorn
roommate
test
video

Verbs
clean
come over
do (the laundry)
dust
eat out
exercise
go jogging
listen (to music)
pay
rent
shop
vacuum
visit
wash

Adverbs
either
else
over

Prepositions
around (the house)
during (the week)
on (the bus)

Interjection
Oh, well.

EXPRESSIONS

Talking about past activities
Did you go out/. . . this weekend?
   Yes, I did. I went to/. . . .
   No, I didn't. I stayed home/. . . .
What did you do?
   I . . . . I didn't . . . .

Giving opinions about past experiences
Did you like . . . ?
   I liked it a lot.
   I loved . . . .
Did you have fun?
   We had a great time.

Asking for additional information
Did you do anything else?

KEY VOCABULARY

Nouns
School subjects
algebra
art
biology
calculus
chemistry
Chinese
computer science
drama
fine arts
French
geometry
history
journalism
languages
mathematics
music
physical education
physical sciences
physics
psychology
social sciences
sociology
Spanish

Other
capital
founder
grade
hairstylist
high school
major
playwright
violinist

Adjectives
fluent
scary

Verbs
be born
become
grow up
promote

Adverb
pretty (young/good)

Preposition
in (college)

EXPRESSIONS

Exchanging personal information
When were you born?
  I was born in . . . .
Where were you born?
  I was born in . . . .
Were you born in . . . ?
  Yes, I was./No, I wasn't. I was born in . . . .
How old were you in . . . ?
  I was . . . .
What was your major in college?
  It was . . . .

Asking about someone
Who was . . . ?
  He was . . . .
What city was he born in?
  He was born in . . . .
What nationality was he?
  He was . . . .
What was he like?
  He was . . . . He wasn't . . . .

Asking for an opinion
What do you think?

PLEASE LEAVE US A MESSAGE.

KEY VOCABULARY

Nouns
art gallery
concert
date
dentist
exam
excuse
(basketball) game
invitation
message
picnic
play
shower
vacation

Pronouns
Object pronouns
me
you *(singular)*
him
her
it
us
you *(plural)*
them

Verbs
baby-sit
call back
give (someone a call)
have to
leave
need to
want to
would like to

Adverb
later

Prepositions
at (the beach)
on (vacation)

Interjection
gee

EXPRESSIONS

Making a phone call
Hello. Is . . . there, please?
  No, I'm sorry, . . . isn't here right now.
  Yes, but . . . can't come to the phone right now.

Recording an answering-machine message
Hi. This is . . . . I/We can't come to the
phone right now. Please leave me/us
a message after the beep.

Leaving a phone message
Please ask . . . to call me.
  Sure, just give me the number.
Hi, it's . . . . Just give me/us a call.

Offering to help someone
Maybe I can help you.

Asking for a favor
Can you . . . ?
Please . . . .

Asking what is happening
What's up?

Inviting and accepting an invitation
Do you want to . . . with me?
  Sure. I'd love to (. . . with you).
  Yes, I'd like to.

**Declining an invitation and
making an excuse**
Do you want to . . . with me?
  I'm sorry, but I can't. I have to . . . .
  Sorry, I need to . . . .
  Gee, I'd like to, but I want to . . . .

Talking about an obligation
I can't . . . . I have to . . . .
  Oh, that's too bad.

Suggesting something
How about . . . ?
  Sure.

Expressing happy surprise
Terrific!

Appendix

ANSWER KEY *Unit 3, Exercise 1, page 14*

Tokyo	**Japan**		Shanghai	**China**
Mexico City	**Mexico**		Los Angeles	**The United States**
São Paulo	**Brazil**		Calcutta	**India**
New York	**The United States**		Buenos Aires	**Argentina**
Bombay	**India**		Seoul	**South Korea**

ANSWER KEY *Unit 3, Exercise 4, page 16*   *Student B*

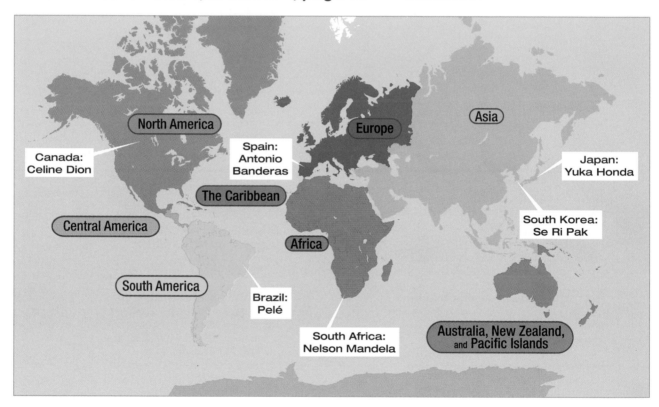

ANSWER KEY *Unit 13, Exercise 7, page 83*

The Golden Gate Bridge: San Francisco   **The Museum of Science and Industry:** Chicago
The White House: Washington, D.C.   **The Statue of Liberty:** New York City

COUNTRIES, NATIONALITIES, AND LANGUAGES

This is a partial list of countries, nationalities, and languages.

Countries	Nationalities	Countries	Nationalities
Argentina	Argentine	Malaysia	Malaysian
Australia	Australian	Mexico	Mexican
Austria	Austrian	Morocco	Moroccan
Bolivia	Bolivian	Nepal	Nepalese
Brazil	Brazilian	the Netherlands	Dutch
Cambodia	Cambodian	New Zealand	New Zealander
Canada	Canadian	Nicaragua	Nicaraguan
Chile	Chilean	Nigeria	Nigerian
China	Chinese	Panama	Panamanian
Colombia	Colombian	Paraguay	Paraguayan
Costa Rica	Costa Rican	Peru	Peruvian
Cuba	Cuban	the Philippines	Filipino
the Dominican Republic	Dominican	Poland	Polish
Ecuador	Ecuadorian	Portugal	Portuguese
Egypt	Egyptian	Puerto Rico	Puerto Rican
El Salvador	El Salvadoran	Russia	Russian
England	English	Saudi Arabia	Saudi
France	French	Singapore	Singaporean
Germany	German	Somalia	Somalian
Ghana	Ghanian	South Africa	South African
Greece	Greek	South Korea	South Korean
Guatemala	Guatemalan	Spain	Spanish
Haiti	Haitian	Sudan	Sudanese
Honduras	Honduran	Sweden	Swedish
India	Indian	Switzerland	Swiss
Indonesia	Indonesian	Tanzania	Tanzanian
Ireland	Irish	Thailand	Thai
Israel	Israeli	Turkey	Turkish
Italy	Italian	the United Kingdom (the U.K.)	British
Japan	Japanese	the United States (the U.S.)	American
Jordan	Jordanian	Uruguay	Uruguayan
Laos	Laotian	Venezuela	Venezuelan
Lebanon	Lebanese	Vietnam	Vietnamese

Languages

Afrikaans	German	Japanese	Spanish
Arabic	Greek	Korean	Swahili
Chinese	Hebrew	Malay	Swedish
Dutch	Hindi	Polish	Thai
English	Indonesian	Portuguese	Turkish
French	Italian	Russian	Vietnamese

IRREGULAR VERBS

Present	Past	Present	Past	Present	Past
(be) am/is, are	was, were	have	had	sing	sang
become	became	know	knew	sit	sat
buy	bought	leave	left	sleep	slept
come	came	make	made	speak	spoke
do	did	meet	met	swim	swam
drink	drank	pay	paid	take	took
drive	drove	read	read /rɛd/	teach	taught
eat	ate	ride	rode	think	thought
feel	felt	run	ran	wear	wore
get	got	say	said /sɛd/	write	wrote
give	gave	see	saw		
go	went	sell	sold		

Acknowledgments

ILLUSTRATIONS

Daisy de Puthod 42 *(top)*
Randy Jones 3 *(bottom)*, 9, 14 *(bottom)*, 20, 21 *(bottom)*, 22, 23 *(bottom)*, 26, 27, 29 *(bottom)*, 30 *(bottom)*, 31, 32, 40 *(bottom)*, 41, 42 *(bottom)*, 43, 46, 52, 53, 56, 68 *(top)*, 73 *(bottom)*, 74, 75, 88, 92, 95, 104 *(top)*, IC-3, IC-6, IC-7, IC-11, IC-13, IC-16, IC-18
Wally Neibart 28 *(bottom)*, 81, 82 *(bottom)*, 104 *(bottom)*, IC-10
Roger Roth 4, 7, 17, 24, 69, 73 *(top)*, 94, IC-5, IC-9
Bill Thomson 2 *(top)*, 3, 5, 28 *(top)*, 34 *(bottom)*, 35, 36, 47, 70, 76, 86 *(bottom)*, 90, 98, 100 *(bottom)*, 102
Daniel Vasconcellos 11, 13, 18, 23 *(top)*, 25, 61, 78, 89 *(bottom)*, 105, IC-14
Sam Viviano 37 *(bottom)*, 50, 62, 63, 66 *(bottom)*, 83, 89 *(top)*

PHOTOGRAPHIC CREDITS

6 *(top)* © Rob Gage/FPG International; *(bottom)* © Telegraph Colour Library/FPG International

8 *(Exercise 1)*: *(pager)* Courtesy of Motorola, Inc.; *(CD player and electronic address book)* © Steven Ogilvy; *(sunglasses, calculator, and cell phone)* © John Bessler; *(watch)* Courtesy of SWATCH Group U.S.; *(camera)* Courtesy of Canon USA, Inc.; *(Exercise 2)*: *(all)* © John Bessler

9 *(television)* © Steven Ogilvy; *(all others)* © John Bessler

10 *(Exercise 5)*: *(CD player)* © Steven Ogilvy; *(all others)* © John Bessler; *(Exercise 6)*: *(umbrella)* © John Bessler; *(chopsticks)* © Steven Ogilvy

12 *(television and CD player, newspaper and map, desk and chair)* © Steven Ogilvy; *(all others)* © John Bessler

15 *(top to bottom)* © Marcus Brooke/FPG International; © Joe Cornish/Tony Stone Images; © John Fuste Raga/The Stock Market

16 *(left to right)* © Benainous/Duclos/Liaison Agency; © Sonia Moscowitz/Globe Photos; © Mark Peters/Liaison Agency; © Evan Agostini/Liaison Agency; © Gamma/Liaison Agency; © AP/Wide World Photos

19 *(top to bottom)* © Adamsmith/FPG International; © James Davis/International Stock; © Gary Buss/FPG International

33 *(clockwise from top left)* © Telegraph Colour Library/FPG International; © Jose Pelaez Photography/The Stock Market; © Chip Simons/FPG International; © Arthur Tilley/FPG International

36 *(left to right)* © Telegraph Colour Library/FPG International; © Ken Reid/FPG International; © Jim Cummins/FPG International; © Jose Luis Banus-March/FPG International

37 © Telegraph Colour Library/FPG International

39 *(left to right)* © Sotographs/Liaison Agency; © VCG/FPG International; © Ken Chernus/FPG International

41 *(left to right)* © E. Alan McGee/FPG International; © Ping Amranand/SuperStock; © Erika Stone; © Chris Springmann/The Stock Market

44 *(top)* © Gerald French/FPG International; *(bottom)* © Robert Shafer/Tony Stone Images

45 *(left)* © Bryce Harper; *(right)* © Steve Northup/NYT Pictures

47 *(left to right)* © Pete Saloutos/The Stock Market; © Jose Pelaez Photography/The Stock Market; © Tom Prettyman/PhotoEdit; © Thomas H. Ives/The Stock Market

48 *(left to right)* © Jose L. Pelaez/The Stock Market; © Don Mason/The Stock Market; © Andy Sacks/Tony Stone Images

49 © Steven Ogilvy

50 *(top to bottom)* © Stephen Simpson/FPG International; © Gary Conner/PhotoEdit; © Bill Stormont/The Stock Market

51 *(top, left to right)* *(chef)* © Dick Luria/FPG International; *(guard)* © Mary Kate Denny/PhotoEdit; *(pilot)* © Tom McCarthy/PhotoEdit; *(bottom, left to right)* © Jose L. Pelaez/The Stock Market; © J. Barry O'Rourke/The Stock Market; © Jose L. Pelaez/The Stock Market

55 © Mark Segal/Tony Stone Images

56 *(all)* © Steven Ogilvy

57 *(both)* © Steven Ogilvy

58 © Jose L. Pelaez/The Stock Market

59 *(all)* © Steven Ogilvy

61 © DiMaggio/Kalish/The Stock Market

62 © Ed Bock/The Stock Market

65 *(all)* © AP/Wide World Photos

67 *(top row, left to right)* © Rob Lewine/The Stock Market; © Michael K. Daly/The Stock Market; © David Stoecklein/The Stock Market; © Jose L. Pelaez/The Stock Market; *(middle row, left)* © DiMaggio/Kalish/The Stock Market; *(middle row, right)* © Don Mason/The Stock Market; *(bottom row, left to right)* © Gary Landsman/The Stock Market; © Telegraph Colour Library/FPG International; © Klaus & Heide Benser/Zefa Germany/The Stock Market; © Michael Newman/PhotoEdit

70 © Steve Vidler/Leo de Wys

71 *(clockwise from top left)* © Roderick Chen/SuperStock; © Bill Walsh/The Stock Market; © Harvey Lloyd/The Stock Market; © David Young-Wolff/PhotoEdit

72 © Steven Ogilvy

74 *(all)* © Steven Ogilvy

77 *(number 3)* © Chris Rogers/The Stock Market; *(number 5)* © David Stoecklein/The Stock Market; *(number 6)* © Roy Morsch/The Stock Market; *(number 7)* © Michael A. Keller Studio/The Stock Market; *(number 8)* © David Raymer/The Stock Market; *(number 9)* © Steven Ogilvy

79 *(top, both)* © Steven Ogilvy; *(bottom)* © Ed Bock/The Stock Market

80 *(aspirin, bread, and sandwich)* © Steven Ogilvy; *(dictionary, stamps, gasoline, and sweatshirt)* © John Bessler; *(bank)* © Charles Orrico/SuperStock; *(drugstore)* © SuperStock; *(bookstore)* © Michael Newman/PhotoEdit; *(gas station)* © Charles Orrico/SuperStock; *(restaurant)* © Rick Rusing/Tony Stone Images; *(post office)* © James P. Dwyer/Stock Boston; *(department store)* © Robert Brenner/PhotoEdit; *(supermarket)* © Chuck Keeler/Tony Stone Images

83 *(clockwise from top left)* © Bruce Hands/Tony Stone Images; © International Stock; © Jean-Marc Truchet/Tony Stone Images; © Dennis O'Clair/Tony Stone Images

85 *(clockwise from top left)* © Fred George/Tony Stone Images; © Andreas Pollok/Tony Stone Images; © Dan Lecca/FPG International; © Thomas A. Kelly/CORBIS

87 © Steven Ogilvy

91 *(left)* © Bettmann/CORBIS; *(right)* © Doug Armand/Tony Stone Images

92 *(clockwise from top left)* © Photofest; © Walter Weissman/Globe Photos; © AFP/CORBIS; © Couponco Worldwide/Liaison Agency

93 © Paul Chesley/Tony Stone Images

94 *(left to right)* © Lisa Rose/Globe Photos; © AP/Wide World Photos; © PHM DeLuigi/M.P.A./Liaison Agency; © Ron Angle/Liaison Agency

97 *(clockwise from top left)* Alexander Calder, *Mobile on Two Planes.* Musée National d'Art Moderne Georges Pompidou Centre, Paris/SuperStock. © 1999 Estate of Alexander Calder/Artists Rights Society (ARS), New York; Frida Kahlo, *Self Portrait With Loose Hair* © Christie's Images/SuperStock. Reproduction authorized by Instituto Nacional de Bellas Artes y Literatura, Mexico; Hiroshigi, *Hida Province (Kago Watashi) Basket Ferry* © Culver Pictures/SuperStock

99 *(left to right)* © SuperStock; © Tony Freeman/PhotoEdit; © R.B. Studio/The Stock Market; © Chuck Savage/The Stock Market; © Philip & Karen Smith/Tony Stone Images

101 © Juan Silva Prod./The Image Bank

102 © Mary Kate Denny/PhotoEdit

103 *(top)* © Robert Brenner/PhotoEdit; *(bottom, left)* © David Young-Wolff/PhotoEdit; *(bottom, right)* © Vittoriano Rastelli/CORBIS

IC-2 and IC-4 © Jim Cummins/FPG International

IC-12 © Steven Ogilvy

IC-15 *(clockwise from top left)* © Gabe Palmer/Mug Shots/The Stock Market; © VCG/FPG International; © Mark Scott/FPG International; © John Terence Turner/FPG International

IC-17 *(clockwise from top right)* © Don Smetzer/Tony Stone Images; © Norbert Schäfer/The Stock Market; © Michael Newman/PhotoEdit; © Myrleen Ferguson Cate/PhotoEdit

IC-20 *(top row, left to right)* Courtesy of Natsu Ifill; © Jonathan Nourok/PhotoEdit; © Paul Barton/The Stock Market; © 100% Rag Productions/FPG International; *(bottom row, left to right)* © Steve Prezant/The Stock Market; © Mike Malyszko/FPG International; Courtesy of Natsu Ifill; © Jose L. Pelaez/The Stock Market

TEXT CREDITS

The authors and publishers are grateful for permission to reprint the following items.

14 *(Snapshot)* http://www.infoplease.com

54 *(Snapshot)* Adapted from the U.S. Department of Agriculture Food Guide Pyramid.

60 *(Snapshot)* Adapted from *1998 ESPN Information Please Sports Almanac*, Copyright © 1997 by Information Please LLC.

74 *(Snapshot)* Adapted from *Almanac of the American People*, Copyright © 1988 by Tom and Nancy Biracree.

77 *(Reading)* Copyright © 1996 *Cooking Light®* Magazine. For subscriptions, call 1-800-336-0125. Reprinted with permission.

83 *(Snapshot)* Adapted from *Fodor's USA*, Copyright © 1998 by Fodor's Travel Publications, Inc.

Thank you to the chef and management of Nadaman Hakubai restaurant at the hotel Kitano New York for their advice on the traditional Japanese breakfast on page 57.

Every effort has been made to trace the owners of copyright material in this book. We would be grateful to hear from anyone who recognizes his or her copyright material and who is unacknowledged. We will be pleased to make the necessary corrections in future editions of the book.